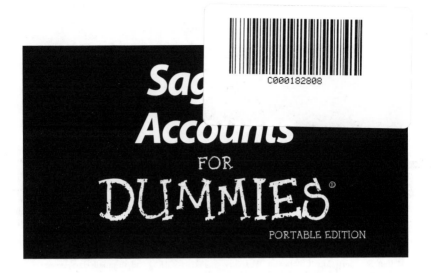

Sage
Accounts
FOR
DUMMIES®

PORTABLE EDITION

by Jane Kelly, ACMA

WILEY

A John Wiley and Sons, Ltd, Publication

Sage 50 Accounts For Dummies®, Portable Edition

Published by
John Wiley & Sons, Ltd
The Atrium
Southern Gate
Chichester
West Sussex
PO19 8SQ
England

E-mail (for orders and customer service enquires): cs-books@wiley.co.uk

Visit our Home Page on www.wiley.com

For general information on our other products and services, please contact our Customer Care Department within the U.S. at 877-762-2974, outside the U.S. at 317-572-3993, or fax 317-572-4002.

For technical support, please visit www.wiley.com/techsupport.

Wiley also publishes its books in a variety of electronic formats. Some content that appears in print may not be available in electronic books.

British Library Cataloguing in Publication Data: A catalogue record for this book is available from the British Library

ISBN: 978-1-119-97446-8 (paperback), ISBN: 978-1-119-97502-1 (ebk), ISBN: 978-1-119-97503-8 (ebk), ISBN: 978-1-119-97504-5 (ebk)

Printed and bound in Great Britain by Bell & Bain Ltd, Glasgow

10 9 8 7 6 5 4 3 2 1

WILEY

About the Author

Jane Kelly trained as a Chartered Management Accountant whilst working in industry. Her roles ranged from Company Accountant in a small advertising business to Financial Controller for a national house-builder. For the last few years Jane has specialised in Sage software as a user and as a Director of a training company. She has taught a variety of small business owners and employees the benefits of using Sage. Jane has written and delivered a range of Sage training courses for both one-to-one and group sessions.

This is Jane's first *For Dummies* book, but won't be the last – she is adapting some US editions for the UK market.

You can keep up to date with Sage news on Jane's blog, at www.sagemadesimple.co.uk.

Dedication

I'd like to dedicate this book to my daughter, Megan. I hope that she'll be proud of her mum and maybe even write a book of her own one day – even if it is about Disney princesses and fairies!

Acknowledgements

I hope that this book will help small businesses who are struggling with their accounting systems. I want people to understand that a properly set up system should be easy to use, and the business will gain maximum benefit from it. In the past, I've only been able to reach small local audiences, but this book gives me the opportunity to reach the masses.

I want to thank everyone at Wiley, who have been incredibly kind and supportive through my first experience of becoming an author. I would like to extend special thanks to Samantha Spickernell who gave me the opportunity to work with Wiley and also to Steve Edwards and his development team who made the book what it is today. I would also like to thank the support team at Sage UK Limited, who provided me with the necessary answers to awkward questions throughout this project. Finally, I would like to thank my husband, Malcolm, and daughter, Megan, who have put up for long periods with an 'absentee wife and mother'.

Publisher's Acknowledgements

We're proud of this book; please send us your comments through our Dummies online registration form located at www.dummies.com/register/.

Some of the people who helped bring this book to market include the following:

Commissioning, Editorial, and Media Development

Project Editor: Steve Edwards

Development Editor: Kathleen Dobie

Content Editor: Jo Theedom

Commissioning Editor: Samantha Spickernell

Publishing Assistant: Jennifer Prytherch

Copy Editor: Anne O'Rorke

Proofreader: Kelly Cattermole

Technical Editor: Rachel Heard

Executive Editor: Samantha Spickernell

Executive Project Editor: Daniel Mersey

Cover Photos: ©Martin Poole/ GettyImages

Cartoons: Ed McLachlan

Composition Services

Project Coordinator: Kristie Rees

Layout and Graphics: Claudia Bell, Timothy C. Detrick, Joyce Haughey, Corrie Socolovitch, Julie Trippetti

Proofreader: Rebecca Denoncour

Indexer: Potomac Indexing, LLC

Contents at a Glance

Table of Contents

Introduction

● ●

*S*age is an accounting system used in more than three quarters of a million small- and medium-sized businesses in the UK. The range of business software continually evolves, and Sage's developers pride themselves on listening to their customers for feedback on how to improve the software. This results in regular revisions and updates that add new features to Sage. This book offers you a chance to understand how Sage 50 Accounts can help you run your business effectively.

About This Book

The aim of this book is for you to get the most from Sage. I use screenshots to help you navigate your way around the system and offer tips to help you customise the Sage programs and reports in language you can understand, even if you're not an accountant. I show you how to navigate your way around Sage, and wherever possible, I show you the easiest or quickest way to do something, because you can often do the same thing in more than one way. I understand that you want a quick start, so I show you the easiest methods of doing things. You can always add details later, when time permits.

This book presents information in a modular fashion so that you get all the information to accomplish a task in one place. I don't ask you to remember things from different parts of the book; if another chapter has information relevant to the discussion at hand, I tell you where to find it, so you don't have to read the chapters in order. You can read the chapters or sections that interest you when it suits you.

Conventions Used in This Book

This book includes a lot of instructions on how to proceed with various tasks in Sage. To help,

- ✔ *Italics* are used to highlight new terms and for emphasis.
- ✔ **Boldfaced** text indicates the action step in a numbered list or text that you type into Sage.
- ✔ Monofont is for web addresses and on-screen messages.
- ✔ Names of windows, screens and menu choices are capitalised.
- ✔ This little arrow – ⇨ – indicates the path you click through in a series of menu options.

Because examples can help you see how a concept works in real life, I created Jingles, a fictitious party-planning company, and I use its owner Jeanette to demonstrate some of Sage's reports and functions.

Foolish Assumptions

I've made assumptions about why you picked up this book, and assume that you fall into one of the following categories:

- ✔ You work in a small business, have been asked to take over the bookkeeping function and will be using Sage.
- ✔ You're an existing bookkeeper who has never used Sage before or who needs to refresh your knowledge.
- ✔ You're a small-business owner who wants to understand how Sage can help in your business.

What You're Not to Read

Throughout *Sage 50 Accounts For Dummies,* I include examples on how to apply processes within your business. If you're simply reading this book to gain an overview of Sage, you can skip these examples without detracting from your understanding of what Sage can do for you and your business.

How This Book Is Organised

Sage 50 Accounts For Dummies is divided into five parts.

Part I: Setting Up and Installing Sage 50 Accounts

Here, I discuss Sage's product range so that you can decide which version best suits your business. I take you through the installation process and help you to navigate around Sage. You see how to set up your Chart of Accounts, records and opening balances so that you can start entering information.

Part II: Looking into Day-to-Day Functions

In these chapters I show you how to process sales and purchase invoices and deal with your bank accounts. I also discuss how to find transactions, how to make corrections and the importance of backing up and restoring data.

Part III: Functions for Plus and Professional Users

Part III is primarily concerned with Sage 50 Accounts Plus and Accounts Professional versions. These two products contain more functions than the standard Sage program, and some of these functions are more advanced. I look at the life cycles of both sales and purchase order processing and the paperwork involved with both. I also look at running a stock system within Sage. If you're interested in setting up projects and their associated costs, Chapter 13 is dedicated to this.

Part IV: Running Monthly, Quarterly and Annual Routines

Here, I look at regular routines that you need to carry out during the year. Some routines are statutory obligations, such as VAT returns, but others are good housekeeping routines. Without reconciling your bank accounts, for example, you can't be certain that you've entered all your bank transactions. I look at the regular journals that you enter if you plan on preparing monthly management information. Finally, I look at reports that you can print out. I show you how to run a Profit and Loss report and a Balance Sheet and discuss which other reports you may like to include in a management accounts pack for the managers and owners of the business to read.

Part V: The Part of Tens

This part contains mini chapters on useful aspects of Sage – ten nifty things to do with function keys and ten best wizards that Sage has to offer.

Icons Used in This Book

For Dummies books use icons to highlight important, interesting or useful information. The icons in this book are:

Look at this icon for practical information that you can use straightaway to help you use Sage in the most effective way.

This icon indicates any items you need to remember after reading the book – and sometimes throughout it.

This icon indicates slightly technical information. You don't *need* to know the information here to get by, but it helps.

This bombshell alerts you to potential problems you may create for yourself without realising it. Don't ignore this icon!

This icon indicates that a function is available only to users of Sage 50 Accounts Plus and Sage 50 Accounts Professional.

Some functions are included only if you run the Professional version of Sage. This icon indicates those functions.

Where to Go from Here

You're now ready to enter the world of Sage. If you're a beginner, starting at the beginning and gradually working through is probably best. However, this book is designed for you to dip in and out of, so if you're an existing user but rusty in places, you can pick chapters that are most relevant to you.

Part I
Setting Up and Installing Sage 50 Accounts

'Mr Scrimshaw, our acccountant, was schooled in the old manual way but I'm sure you two will enjoy working together on a new computerised system.'

In this part . . .

I introduce the product range and help you decide which product is going to be the most useful to you. I tell you how to install the software and what information you need beforehand. I take you step by step through setting up your records and Chart of Accounts and show you how to navigate around the system.

Finally, you discover how to enter and check your opening balances. You're then ready to rock and roll!

Chapter 1

Introducing Sage 50 Accounts

*I*n this chapter, I introduce you to the Sage 50 Accounts software range. I show you how easily you can install the software and give you a guided tour, so that you can get up and running quickly – essential for busy people! Sage works on the principle that the less time you spend doing your accounts, the more time you can spend on your business, so makes each process is as simple as possible.

Looking at the Varieties of Sage

Sage's developers understand that every business is different and that each business has different needs. As a result, they've developed a range of accounting software designed to grow with your business, whatever it is. The three levels of Sage 50 Accounts software start with basic features and finish with a product that contains all the bells and whistles you can possibly want! These versions of Sage are:

✔ **Sage 50 Accounts:** The entry-level program. Sage 50 Accounts provides all the features you require to successfully manage your accounts. You can professionally handle your customers and suppliers, manage your bank reconciliations and VAT returns, and provide simple reports, including monthly and year-end requirements. This basic version is suitable for small businesses with a simple structure; those that need basic stock systems, and don't need systems project costing, foreign currency or sales/purchase order processing.

✔ **Sage 50 Accounts Plus:** Contains all the features of the entry model and enables you to manage project costs versus budgets, control costs of manufactured and assembled products, and has an improved stock control system that you can use to produce bill of materials and allocate stock.

✔ **Sage 50 Accounts Professional:** Includes all the features of Accounts Plus and adds sales and purchase order processing, foreign trading, bank account revaluation and Intrastat support. Accounts Professional can also handle up to ten users and manage multiple companies. This product is suited to both small- and medium-sized businesses and offers customers a product flexible enough to suit a multitude of different businesses, including those who trade in both the UK and abroad.

Sage is best installed on a Windows operating system. XP is recommended, but Sage also works on Windows Vista, the latest Windows operating system. Installation on Apple operating systems isn't recommended (that's not to say that Sage doesn't work on Macs, it just hasn't been tested to the same extent).

Deciding on SageCover

You can purchase SageCover at the same time you buy the software. SageCover provides you with technical support in case you have any problems using Sage. It may seem an additional cost burden to begin with, but it's well worth the money if you have a software problem. To find out more, visit the Sage website at www.sage.co.uk and click on the 'Sage Store' tab.

Installing the Software

The Sage Installation process is very simple. After loading the CD which is supplied with the software, you're taken through a series of self-explanatory steps.

You're given the choice of either a Standard Install, which is recommended, or a Custom Install, which is only suitable if you want to control the destination of the programs being installed (see Figure 1-1).

Figure 1-1: Choosing Standard or Custom install.

When you've made your choice, the system whirrs into action and starts the installation process. This takes several minutes, so you probably have time to make a quick cup of tea! Sage prompts you when the installation is complete, and you should now see a Sage 50 Accounts icon on your desktop. Now you're ready to rock and roll!

Be sure to remove the CD and keep it in a safe place!

Having a Practice

Of course, you're champing at the bit and want to get going with Sage, so double-click the new Sage icon on your desktop. As this is the first time you're opening Sage 50 Accounts, you're asked to select the type of data that you want to use. Figure 1-2 shows the screen that poses this question.

If you're likely to be annoyed by seeing the Select the Type of Data You Want to Use window every time you open Sage, tick the Don't Show These Options On Start Up box and click OK to stop the window from opening each time.

Figure 1-2: Choosing your data options from the Select the Type of Data You Want to Use screen.

Choose an option according to your interest:

- ✔ **Open Practice Data:** The practice company doesn't have any actual data to start with, but you can enter dummy data, for example, new records and dummy invoices, to see how the transactions are posted to the different parts of the system. Tutorials help you get familiar with Sage.

- ✔ **Open Demonstration Data:** This option has some dummy company information already entered. You can use this data to navigate around the system and see how transactions are presented.

If you select one of the options above and click OK, the Sage Logon window appears, as shown in Figure 1-3. Type **manager** (not case sensitive), leave the password blank and click OK. Sage opens, using whichever data type you chose. Then click Start Practising.

Figure 1-3: The Sage Logon window.

In future, if you need to use the practice company or demo data, you can select File and then Open from the main toolbar.

If you want to jump straight in without using any of the practice data, continue to the next section.

Setting Up with the Active Set-Up Wizard

When you click the Sage icon on your desktop, the Select the Type of Data You Want to Use window appears (see Figure 1-2). If you decide you don't fancy using either of the practice options, you can click Set up your Company Data to open the Active Set-up wizard. You are then given three options:

- ✔ **Set up a new company:** If you're new to Sage, choose this first option. You're guided through the automatic steps of the Active Set-up wizard.

- ✔ **Use a company already set up in another installation:** If you already use Sage and are upgrading, choose this option, which lets you copy accounts data from your previous Sage installation.

- ✔ **Restore data from a backup file:** Choose this option if you're restoring data from an earlier version – no earlier than Version 9 – perhaps from your accountant, to use in your new Sage installation.

Choose whichever option is best for you and follow the screen prompts. Now that you're in the Active Set-up wizard, Sage will guide you step-by-step through the process of setting up your company information. Once again, the steps are very self- explanatory. The information that you need available is:

- ✔ Company contact details and type of business

- ✔ Start date of your financial year (ask your accountant if you're not sure when this is)

- ✔ Your VAT number (assuming you're VAT registered)

- ✔ Your currency (for most people this is sterling)

Towards the end of the wizard, you're asked for your Serial Number and Activation Key. These will have been sent to you with the Sage software. The final screen summarises the data you entered on your Active Set-up wizard. If you need to make any changes to your data, you can click Back and revise any information. Select Finish when you're satisfied that the information is correct.

Registering Your Software

After you install Sage, you may get a message telling you that you're using an unregistered version of the program. Don't panic! You have 60 days before you are required to formally register. You need to contact Sage (UK), Ltd, directly to obtain a new activation key; your serial number remains the same. You can register by phoning the Sage Customer Care Helpline at 0845 1116666 or by visiting the Sage website at www.sage. co.uk and clicking on the Support and Training tab. Follow the online instructions to register your software.

Finding Out How Easy Sage Is to Use

Sage is a user-friendly system, using words and phrases that people easily understand rather than accounting jargon. Sage also has a lot of graphics to make the pages look more appealing and easier to navigate. For example, an icon appears next to the Bank module that looks like the entrance to a grand building – like the Bank of England, perhaps?

Burying the accounting jargon

Sage uses terms that users understand and steers clear of accounting jargon. So, instead of using *debtors* and *creditors*, Sage uses *customers* and *suppliers;* rather than *nominal ledger*, it uses *company*. Accounting terminology isn't altogether done away with, though. For example, you still print Aged Debtors reports and Aged Creditors reports, but the front end of the program uses very simple language.

Introducing process maps

Sage introduced process maps a while back. These maps look like flow charts and they illustrate specific customer and supplier processes in a pictorial format. Figure 1-4 shows the various stages of the customer paper trail in the Customer Process map, from the original quotation through to chasing the debt and receiving the money from the customer. You can click any one of these boxes, and Sage takes you directly to the screen necessary to process that action. For example, if you click Receive Payment, you're taken to the Customer Receipt screen, so that you can process the payment received.

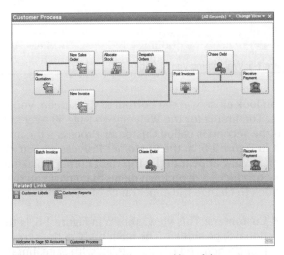

Figure 1-4: Looking at the inner working of the customer process.

Looking at the screen layout

When you open Sage, the first screen you come across is the Sage Welcome screen, as shown in Figure 1-5. It provides useful links to the websites and various Help pages, including a page that shows you what's new in Sage 50 Accounts.

Figure 1-5: Welcoming you to Sage.

If you look closely at the bottom of the screen, you find two tabs. The first is for the Welcome to Sage 50 Accounts screen, and the second is called Customer Process – the arrow points to it in Figure 1-5. In the Customer Process screen, the words Change View appear in the top right corner. Clicking Change View produces a dropdown menu that gives you two more options to change the appearance of the screen:

✔ **Customers:** This view, shown in Figure 1-6, is the traditional Sage screen. The main body of the screen appears blank when you're starting out with Sage, but it eventually fills up with your customer names, balances and contact details. Across the top of the screen, below the Customer heading, the icons that form part of the customer pages appear – Activity, Invoice and Credit, to name just a few.

✔ **Customer Dashboard**: The dashboard offers a graphic representation of the customer information. It shows the Customer Cash Overview, Aged Debt, Promised Payments and Today's Diary Events. This presentation appeals to top management, who want quick access to the key information in the accounts.

Navigating Around Sage

At the very top of the Sage Welcome screen is the name of your version of Sage – Sage 50 Accounts Professional 2011, for example – followed by the company name you entered when you set up Sage. (Refer to the 'Setting Up with the Active Set-Up Wizard' section, which walks you through getting Sage up and running.)

From the Welcome screen, use the browser toolbar that runs horizontally across the top to navigate through the program. For example, if you misspelled your company name in your excitement at setting up, or missed off *Ltd*, you can amend the error by using the browser toolbar.

Exploring the browser toolbar

The browser toolbar is the traditional way of navigating around the system. Sage introduced the navigation bar that runs down the left side of the screen more recently. (Refer to Figure 1-6 to see both the browser toolbar and navigation bar.) The navigation bar includes the Task pane, Links list and Module buttons (see 'Navigating the Task pane, Links list and Module buttons' later in this chapter for more detail).

The browser toolbar gives you access to submenus and different parts of the system. Take some time to familiarise yourself with this toolbar. If you struggle trying to find anything, then click Help and type in your question. Rather than detail every item in the toolbar, I've selected the most useful ones to look at in the following sections:

File

Submenu options available to you here include:

- **Backup**: Allows you to back up your data. You can also back up your data when you exit the program.

  Back up your data each time you use Sage, or at least at the end of each day. Back up more often during the day if you're processing significant amounts of data.

Sage automatically gives the backup a filename, which is usually SageBack DD-MM-YY.001. (Sage backup files always have the file extension .001.) If you do more than one backup on the same day, differentiate the file name, otherwise Sage uses the same date and the same file name and simply overwrites the previous backup.

✔ **Import:** Allows you to import records, such as customer records, stock records and project records, from other sources, like Microsoft Excel, as long as they're in a pre-determined CSV (comma separated values) format. This option is useful when you're setting up Sage and have other information or records that you wish to import. You can speed up the data-entry process if you import information instead of keying in each individual record.

✔ **Maintenance:** Enables you, amongst other things, to correct data, delete records, check data or even, as a very last resort, rebuild the data. I talk about maintenance in more detail in Chapter 9.

✔ **Restore:** Enables you to retrieve data from a previous backup if necessary. You may need to do this if you have problems with the current data – perhaps the data had become corrupted and you want to return the data to a known point in time when the data was problem-free.

Modules

The *modules* are essentially the different components that form the whole of the Sage accounting system. The modules include the usual accounting ledgers, such as Customers, Suppliers, Bank, Nominal Ledger and reporting functions, but they also include (depending on which version of Sage you purchased) additional components, such as Projects, Sales Order Processing and Purchase Order Processing. You can also access the Invoicing function, wizards, a diary and a button for Sage Services. This gives you the ability to access other parts of Sage from the Internet. You need to set up your Sage Passport details via the Configure Settings option to be able to benefit from the full functionality.

Access modules by clicking Modules on the browser toolbar and selecting the module of your choice, or by clicking the much larger buttons on the navigation bar at the bottom left side of the screen. I prefer the buttons at the bottom – they're easier to use and more visible.

Settings

The settings include the Configuration Editor and Company Preferences, which hold some basic information about your company and the way Sage was set up upon installation. Settings also include many of the default screens for the ledgers, which save you time when setting up records later on. If you need to change the system date or check the financial year, you can do it within settings. You also have access to the security settings for accessing the software and can set up passwords to protect your accounts data. The settings include:

- ✔ **Configuration Editor:** Holds the basic information you enter when you complete the Active Set-up wizard. Have a look at the numerous tabs within this option and familiarise yourself with them. Examples of things you can do include: editing your customer and supplier trading terms; amending your VAT codes; and managing your project cost types and cost codes.

- ✔ **Company Preferences:** Allows you to enter extra information if you didn't add it all when using the Active Set-up wizard. You may want to update your address information. Company Preferences provides many more tabs to look at, too many to comment on here, so have a flick through at your leisure.

- ✔ **Customer/Supplier/Bank/Product/Invoice and Order Defaults:** Gives you the opportunity to amend parts of the default data you set up on installation.

- ✔ **Financial Year:** Identifies the start of the company's financial year, as input during the Active Set-up wizard. This date is fixed when you start to enter data.

- ✔ **Change Program Date:** Allows you to change dates when running a month-end or a year-end report. The date is normally set to the current day's date, but there may be times, such as period ends, when you wish to change the date, albeit only temporarily.

Tools

The tools option is a hotchpotch of items. You can run the Global Changes wizard, carry out contra entries, run period ends, open up Report Designer and convert reports, to name but a few. Other options include:

✓ **Period End:** Enables you to run the month-end, allowing you to post accruals, prepayments and depreciation. This option also clears the current-month turnover figures. You can run your year-end, which sets your Profit and Loss nominal accounts to zero for the new financial year.

✓ **Options:** Gives you options to change the settings and appearance of Sage. For example, you can change the default view of the Customers and Suppliers screens from the process map to customer or supplier lists.

Help

Help is the last entry on the browser toolbar, but probably one of the most useful. If you want to understand more about the system and want to know how to do something, click the Help option. The Contents and Index option allows you to type in key words that may help with answering your question.

Navigating the Task pane, Links list and Module buttons

An alternative method of navigation, and probably the easiest, is to use the navigation bar, which is down the left side of the screen. It includes a Task pane and Links list, as well as buttons at the bottom of the bar for opening up your modules.

As you may have gathered by now, Sage offers a variety of ways to navigate to the same point. For example, if you want to open a new customer record, you can click New Customer in the Task pane or use the browser toolbar and click Modules, Customers and then the New icon (assuming you've changed the view to Customers and haven't left it on the process map – refer to the 'Looking at the screen layout' section earlier in this chapter).

As you get used to using Sage, you'll see that the first navigation bar to open is the Customers bar. Figure 1-6 shows the navigation bar in the Customer module, where you can see these features:

✓ **Task pane:** The topmost menu is the Task pane, which is different for each module.

✓ **Links list:** The Links list offers different links for each module within Sage. The Customer Links list takes you to customer-orientated pages, such as Customer Invoices, Orders or simply a list of customers.

✔ **Module buttons:** These wide buttons sit at the bottom left of the screen and enable you to switch between modules. They start with a little icon and a description. The first button is Customers, the next is Suppliers, then Company, Bank, Products, Projects and Diary. Just below the Diary button is a tiny chevron with a small arrow directly beneath it. Clicking the chevron gives you the option of showing fewer buttons or adding or removing buttons. You can play about with the buttons and decide which display you prefer. (The Diary button is a new feature recently added to Sage. It assists with credit control and is discussed in Chapter 6 in more detail.)

Clicking the tasks, links or Module buttons moves you to the relevant part of the system. I prefer the Module buttons, finding it easier to navigate with them as they're more visible and easier to click than the Task pane or Links list.

Figure 1-6: Identifying the Navigation bar, the Task pane, the Links list, the Module buttons, and the two toolbars as viewed from the Customers module.

Using Wizards

A number of wizards wield their technological magic through Sage. You can access these helpful creatures, whose job is to help you through a wide variety of set-ups and tasks, by clicking Modules on the browser toolbar and then Wizards.

A wizard's work is to make your work easy; all you have to do is follow the prompts and enter the information the wizard requests. See Chapter 19 for more details about wizards.

Chapter 2

Creating Your Chart of Accounts and Assigning Nominal Codes

$\bullet$

In This Chapter

▶ Getting familiar with some accounting concepts

▶ Charting your accounts

▶ Adding nominal codes in your Chart of Accounts

▶ Changing your Chart of Accounts

$\bullet$

*I*n this chapter, I get down to the nitty-gritty of the accounting system – the Chart of Accounts (COA), which is made up of nominal codes. Think of the Chart of Accounts as the engine of the accounting system. From the information in your COA, you produce your Profit and Loss report, your Balance Sheet, your budget report and prior-year reports. Set it up properly, and the Chart of Accounts grows with your business, but set it up wrongly and you'll have problems forever more!

Luckily, Sage gives you a lot of help and does the hard work for you, but you still need to understand why Sage is structured in the way that it is and how you can customise it to suit your business.

Understanding as Much as You Need to about Accounting

To use Sage, it helps if you have an appreciation of accounts and understand what you're trying to achieve. But you certainly don't need to understand all the rules of double-entry bookkeeping. The next sections give you the basics of accounting principles so that you can use Sage more comfortably.

Dabbling in double-entry bookkeeping

Accounting systems and accounting programs such as Sage use the principle of *double-entry bookkeeping*, so called because each transaction is recorded twice. For every debit entry, you record a corresponding credit entry. Doing the two entries helps balance the books.

Some knowledge of double-entry rules helps. That way, you can interpret information a little more easily. Fortunately, though, you don't need to book yourself into a bookkeeping evening class, as Sage does the double-entry for you . . . phew! (If you're intrigued by the double-entry system though, please pick up a copy of *Bookkeeping For Dummies* by Paul Barrow and Lisa Epstein, published by Wiley, which explains double-entry and more.)

Having said that, understanding the double-entry method does help, particularly if you intend to do your own nominal journals. This knowledge also comes in handy if you intend to produce monthly management accounts. Sometimes, you need to post nominal journals to correct mistakes, and understanding the principles of double-entry bookkeeping lets you confidently process journals. Don't panic though – Sage has many wizards, which can post things like depreciation, accruals and prepayments for you. So some familiarity with the double-entry method is important, but thorough knowledge isn't essential. If you struggle with journals, leave them to your accountant or at least seek advice if you aren't sure.

Naming your nominals

In accounting and in Sage, you bump into the term *nominal* quite a bit. And for good reason, as several key concepts use the word:

> ✔ **Nominal account:** Every item of income, expense, asset and liability is posted to a Nominal Ledger account. The Nominal Ledger accounts categorise all your transactions. The individual nominal accounts are grouped into ranges and can be viewed in your Chart of Accounts.

> ✔ **Nominal code:** A four-digit number given to each account that appears in the nominal ledger. For example, 7502 is the nominal code for telephone expenses, which is an account in the nominal ledger.

> Sage categorises each nominal code into nine different ranges, and these categories form the basis of your Chart of Accounts.

> ✔ **Nominal ledger:** The nominal ledger is an accumulation of all the nominal accounts – it's the main body of the accounting system. Each nominal account shows all the transactions posted to that specific code, so it follows that the nominal ledger represents all the transactions of the business in one place. Deep joy, I hear you say!

> Sage tries to complicate things by referring to the nominal ledger as Company.

> ✔ **Nominal record:** An individual record for each nominal code. So, to create a new nominal code, open up a new nominal record and give it the new nominal code as its reference. See Chapter 3 for more details about nominal records.

The Profit and Loss and Balance Sheet reports are created from the information in the Chart of Accounts, so it's important to get the COA right!

I discuss the Profit and Loss report and Balance Sheet more fully in Chapter 17, where I also cover producing monthly accounts and the types of reports you're likely to need.

Looking at the Structure of Your Chart of Accounts (COA)

The Chart of Accounts, or COA, is in the Company module (see Figure 2-1). To display it, click Modules on the main (browser) toolbar and then select Company, or simply click the Company button from the navigation bar down the left side of the screen. (Make sure that you click Show More Buttons at the bottom of the navigation bar so that all the buttons are visible).

Figure 2-1: Going through the Nominal Ledger to get to the Chart of Accounts.

Essentially, the Chart of Accounts is a list of nominal codes, divided up into the nine categories below:

- ✔ Fixed Assets
- ✔ Current Assets
- ✔ Current Liabilities
- ✔ Long-term Liabilities
- ✔ Capital and Reserves

  ✔ Sales

  ✔ Purchases

  ✔ Direct Expenses

  ✔ Overhead

The first five categories form the Balance Sheet; the remaining categories create your Profit and Loss report. So the COA is a pretty important part of the system!

A look at the nominal list on the Nominal Ledger screen shows that the list runs in numerical order, with the Balance Sheet codes first.

Checking out the default COA

Being a caring, sharing software developer, Sage provides a default Chart of Accounts for you to use, with a ready-made list of nominal codes. (You select the type of COA you want using the Active Set-up wizard, which I go through in Chapter 1.) Your COA is determined by the type of business you operate. For most businesses, the default Chart of Accounts based on the general business type is the most appropriate, and it's the one I use here.

Whilst Sage can spot if a new nominal code is outside the range of the usual Chart of Accounts, it can't really help with the structure of the coding system that you choose to use, so plan ahead to avoid costly mistakes.

For a better look at the Chart of Accounts screen, you can click on the COA icon shown circled in Figure 2-1.

If you double click Default Layout of Accounts, the Edit Chart of Accounts box will appear as shown in Figure 2-2. This screen shows the category types on the left side and a description of the nominal code ranges contained within each category on the right side.

As you click each category type, the nominal codes shown in the Category Account window change to match the category type. Have a go and see for yourself.

Figure 2-2: Looking at the Edit Chart of Accounts window.

In the Category Account window, all you see is nominal code ranges. For example, in Figure 2-2, Sales is highlighted in the Description column of the category type, so the Category Account columns show the High and Low ranges of nominal codes within each Sales category. I explain the nominal code ranges in the next two sections.

If you're not sure which nominal codes fall into the range described, you can print a complete list of nominal codes. Alternatively, you can click the number in the Low or High column and use the dropdown arrow next to the field to see which account the nominal code is referring to. You can then scroll down the list of accounts that appear and view the range of codes.

The list of nominal codes may look rather daunting at first, but I talk you through the basics in the next sections.

Identifying Balance Sheet codes

The *Balance Sheet* is a snapshot of the business at a fixed point in time. It identifies the company's assets and liabilities and shows how the business has been funded via the capital accounts. To achieve this snapshot, the Balance Sheet looks at the assets the business holds and its liabilities, so it draws on the numbers in a range of nominal codes:

- ✓ **Fixed assets (0010–0051):** A *fixed asset* is an item likely to be held in the business for a long period of time – more than 12 months. The range of fixed-asset codes is used for transactions relating to freehold and leasehold property, and other items the company plans to hold for a while. You can add other capital items, such as computer equipment, to this list.

✓ **Current assets (1001–1250):** A *current asset* is an item that has a lifespan of 12 months or less. You should be able to *liquidate* (turn into cash) current assets reasonably quickly. Common current assets include stock, debts owed to the business, and bank and cash items. Current assets are normally ordered in the least liquid order first, meaning items that take the longest to convert into cash appear at the top of the list. Therefore you expect to see cash, which is so liquid it runs through some people's hands like water, at the bottom of the current assets list.

✓ **Current liabilities (2100–2230):** *Current liabilities* are amounts the business owes normally outstanding for less than 12 months. At the top of the list is the Creditors control account, which is basically the total owed to all suppliers. But it also includes amounts owed to HM Revenue and Customs, which include VAT and PAYE, if applicable.

✓ **Long-term liabilities (2300–2330):** These liabilities are amounts owed by the business for a period of more than 12 months. They include long-term loans, hire-purchase agreements and mortgages.

✓ **Capital (3000–3200):** Capital accounts show how the business is funded. These codes include those for share issues, reserves and the current Profit and Loss balance.

Reserves is another word for earnings retained within the business – they're officially called *retained earnings*. Annual profits swell this account and any distributions of dividends to owners of the business reduce the balance.

In order for the Balance Sheet to balance, the Capital account includes the current-year profit, as shown in the Profit and Loss report.

Looking at profit and loss codes

In the default set of nominal codes, all codes from 4000 onwards are Profit and Loss codes, which, appropriately enough, include the numbers that show how much money the business brings in and how much it spends. The Profit and Loss codes include the following:

✔ **Sales (4000–4999):** Sales codes apply to goods or services that your business offers; they indicate how you earn your money. The 4000–4999 range also includes income other than sales, for example, royalty commissions.

The default descriptions against the sales codes are nonsense. Sales Type A, B, C, D and so on are not meaningful to anyone; they're just a starting point. You need to change the sales types to make them applicable for your business. If you own a card shop, for example, instead of Sales type A, you may have nominal code (N/C) 4000 for birthday cards, sales type B may become N/C 4005 for get-well cards, and so on. I look at editing nominal codes in Chapter 3.

✔ **Purchases (5000–5299):** These codes identify material purchases and purchasing costs such as carriage, packaging and transport insurance. *Material purchases* is a very general term for the purchase of the raw materials used to make the products the business sells. For example, flour is a material purchase for a bakery.

✔ **Direct Expenses (6000–6999):** A *direct expense* is a cost directly associated with the product being manufactured or created by the business. Labour costs, including subcontractors, come under these codes, which also include expenses such as sales commissions, samples and public relations costs that can be associated directly with the products.

✔ **Overheads (7000–9999):** By far the largest range of codes is *overheads,* which covers all other expenses not directly associated with making and providing the products or service.

Leaving gaps and mirroring codes

Notice that the ranges of codes in the preceding sections leave plenty of gaps between the categories. For example, Sales codes start at 4000 and the next range of Purchase codes doesn't begin until 5000. You can fill the large gap between 4000 and 4999 with Sales codes, which gives you a great deal of flexibility for a growing business.

I suggest leaving gaps of ten between each code to allow for growth, but it's entirely up to you to decide the best fit for your business. You may decide that gaps of 50 are quite sufficient.

You may consider mirroring corresponding Sales and Purchase codes, so that the last two digits are the same for the sale and purchase of each item, as in Table 2-1, which shows some of Jingles' nominal codes. (Jingles is the fictional card shop and party-planning company I created to serve as an example throughout this book.)

Table 2-1	Mirroring Nominal Codes		
Nominal Code	*Description*	*Nominal Code*	*Description*
4000	Sale of greetings cards	5000	Purchase of greetings cards
4010	Sale of party balloons	5010	Purchase of party balloons
4020	Sale of party gifts	5020	Purchase of party gifts

Accommodating floating nominals

A *floating nominal* is a code that can be placed as a Current Asset or Current Liability, depending on whether the balance is a debit or a credit. For example, if your bank account is in the black, it's a Current Asset, but if the account is overdrawn, it should show as a Current Liability. Another example is the VAT Liability account, as you can sometimes get a refund from the Inland Revenue.

The Sage program automatically places the code to the correct side of the Balance Sheet, but only if you've identified those specific codes that can be treated as an asset or as a liability in the Floating Nominal Accounts section on the Edit Chart of Accounts screen. Sage normally designates accounts as floating nominal codes, so you don't have to do anything.

Editing Your Chart of Accounts

One of the first things to consider when setting up Sage is how well the Chart of Accounts suits your business. Have a look at the categories and nominal codes to make sure that they contain suitable descriptions for your products or services. For example, the Product Sales category doesn't suit a business that primarily provides a service. You may want to change a few categories, or you may decide to make wholesale changes, in which case it may be simpler to create an entirely new Chart of Accounts. The next sections tell you how to change and create COAs.

If you place a nominal code in the wrong category, it can cause inaccuracies in the reports you produce; miscodings are every accountant's nightmare! When creating new codes, be sure that you know whether the code should be a Balance Sheet or a Profit and Loss item. You can usually rely on your common sense, but if you're unsure, give your accountant a quick call. Accountants don't mind answering a quick question like this, but they do mind if you mix up Balance Sheet and Profit and Loss codes, and they then have the task of unpicking your mistakes!

Amending your Chart of Accounts

You can edit the default Chart of Accounts to suit your business.

In Figure 2-2 (in the earlier 'Checking out the default COA' section), the category types are on the left side of the screen, starting with Profit and Loss items and followed by Balance Sheet items. If you move your cursor down the list of sales types, the Sales account headings on the right side of the screen change to reflect the heading names and nominal codes contained within the highlighted category types. To view the nominal code ranges in more detail, click the nominal code and then use the dropdown arrow to identify the name of the nominal code.

Don't change the category types on the left side of the COA screen: they are fundamental accounting descriptions, and the layout of both the Profit and Loss report and Balance Sheet should conform with recognised financial reporting standards.

However, you can change the category accounts on the right side of the Edit Chart of Accounts page. The headings aim to describe the group of nominal codes linked under the heading.

One of the first things to change is the Product Sales headings. These headings are very general descriptions and won't suit all business. For example, if you're a baker using Sage, you may want to change the sales types to bread sales, cake sales and so on.

The headings in the Chart of Accounts show up in your Profit and Loss report and Balance Sheet, so you need to give careful consideration to which headings you want to see on your financial reports. If you don't want an extensive list of different types of sales categories on your Profit and Loss account, consider grouping together several nominal codes under more general headings.

After you decide on the level of detail that you want to show on your reports, you're now ready to amend your Chart of Accounts by following these steps:

1. **From the navigation bar, click Company and then click COA.**

2. **Make sure that you highlight Default Layout of Accounts and then click Edit.**

3. **Make any changes to headings within the category account.**

   Changes available are:

   - **Rename a heading:** Simply click the title and overtype with the new name.

   - **Insert a new heading:** Click the line below where you want to insert a line and press the F7 function key. A message comes up to say that inserting a line moves all categories down by one. Click Yes and don't panic when the codes above disappear from view! They're still there, they've just moved up. Scroll up the category accounts to see where your line has been inserted. Type the name of the new heading and then enter the range of nominal codes to which it relates.

• **Delete a heading:** You can use F8 to delete a heading line, but you must ensure that you're not likely to want to use those nominal codes.

4. **Click Save when you're happy with the changes you've made.**

You need to go through your Chart of Accounts for errors, so check out the 'Checking your Chart of Accounts' section later in this chapter.

Creating a new Chart of Accounts

If the existing Chart of Accounts doesn't suit your business at all, you may find that creating your own COA is less work than adapting the one Sage provides. You may decide to use your existing nominal codes from your old accounting system, so you can customise the Chart of Accounts with your existing codes.

To add a Chart of Accounts, follow these steps:

1. **From the navigation bar, select the Company module and click COA.**

2. **Click Add from the COA window.**

The New Chart of Accounts window appears.

3. **Enter the name of your new Chart of Accounts and click Add.**

4. **Select each category type by clicking the Description field and entering a description in the Category Account on the right side of the screen.**

5. **Use the Category Account pane on the right side of the screen to enter new headings and assign a range of codes for each heading.**

Also, if you want just one code within the range, then the code is the same in both the High and Low columns.

Deleting a Chart of Accounts

You may find that while you've been playing around designing new Charts of Accounts, you created too many variations and want to delete some of them.

Follow these steps:

1. **Click Company and then Chart of Accounts.**

   The Chart of Accounts window opens.

2. **Highlight the Chart of Accounts that you want to delete and click Delete.**

3. **Click Yes to confirm that you want to delete it.**

   If you decide that you don't want to delete, click No and return to the main Chart of Accounts window.

Checking Your Chart of Accounts

After you make any changes to your Chart of Accounts, you need to ensure that your COA doesn't contain any errors. If an error is present, the Profit and Loss or Balance Sheet reports may be incorrect, and a warning message flashes up every time you run these reports.

To check your Chart of Accounts, follow these steps:

1. **Go to the Company module and click COA.**

2. **Click Edit.**

3. **Click Check.**

If no problems are present, Sage tells you that no errors were found in the Chart of Accounts, and you can breathe a sigh of relief. However, if a little window entitled Chart of Accounts Errors appears, be prepared to take corrective action.

Previewing errors

The Chart of Accounts Errors window enables you to send the report directly to your printer or to simply preview, save to a new location or email. to someone.

Usually, the best method is to preview the report first, to make sure that it's providing you with the information you expected, and then you can print a hard copy if you like what you see.

Looking at some common errors

Whenever you add new nominal codes, the chance exists that they may not fit within the nominal code structure currently in place. This common oversight leads to errors within the COA.

Common errors include:

- ✓ **Overlapping ranges:** The same nominal code occurs in two different ranges and is therefore counted twice.

- ✓ **Enclosing one range within another range:** Assigning a range of codes that's within another range is a big no-no.

- ✓ **Using a floating code in one category but not in its complementary category:** You may require a floating code so that an item such as the Bank account can be both a Current Asset or a Current Liability, depending on whether the account is overdrawn or not. If you set up a floating code in Current Assets but not in Current Liabilities or vice versa, you get an error message.

Chapter 3

Setting Up Records

● ●

In This Chapter

▶ Choosing a quick start or step by step

▶ Setting up records for customers and suppliers

▶ Registering your bank accounts

▶ Accounting for your products

▶ Depreciating your fixed assets

● ●

*A*fter you install your Sage software, you quickly realise that the hard work is only just beginning! You now have to create the records necessary to operate your accounting system, including creating records for your customers and suppliers and your existing bank accounts. Depending on your business, you may also need to set up stock and project records. This chapter tells you how.

Choosing How to Create Your Records

Setting up records may seem a daunting task, but Sage provides at least two ways of doing things: a quick way, using the Record icon within the relevant module and the step-by-step way, which involves using the wizards. If you like the belt and braces approach, choose the wizards, as they help you complete each section of the record thoroughly. However, if you're a bit of a speed freak and want to get on with things as quickly as possible, and don't mind leaving a few less important data fields blank (you can always update them later), choose the quick start option outlined in the next section. I always use this method, as time is always of the essence.

Getting a quick start using the Record icon

If you're looking for a quick start, the first thing you need to do is locate the Record icon. To set up records for nominal accounts, bank accounts, products and projects, click the relevant Module button from the navigation bar, and you're presented with the associated icons for each module, including the Record icon. You can also click the relevant Edit option on the Task pane for each module. A record opens for you to start entering data.

For customer and supplier records, after you click the module button from the navigation bar, you're presented with a process map, which is currently the default screen. If you want to switch the process maps off, see the following section.

If you want to keep the Process screen as your default screen, the easiest way to set up a new customer or supplier record is to the use the New Customer or New Supplier wizard in the Task Pane. Alternatively, you can click on Customer List (on Links List) and this will bring up the Customer Ledger, where you can click on the Record icon to set up a new customer/supplier.

Switching off the process maps

If you want to switch off the process maps and see the Customers or Suppliers screen instead, follow these steps:

1. **From the main toolbar, click Tools.**

2. **Select Options.**

3. **Click Yes to the confirmation screen, if you have other windows open.**

4. **In the Options menu, select the View tab. Click the small dropdown arrow next to Customers Process Maps and select Customers List. Do the same for Suppliers.**

5. **Click OK.**

Now, as soon as you enter either the customer or the supplier ledger, the default screen shows the icons. You can click the Record icon to create as many records as you require. See the 'Creating Customer and Supplier Records' section later in this chapter.

Creating Customer and Supplier Records

Because setting up customer and supplier records is essentially the same process, I cover both of them in this section. Wizards can walk you through creating both types of records (just click New in the relevant module), but for the quick start method, read on:

Click the Record icon using one of the methods outlined in the preceding 'Getting a Quick Start using the Record Icon' section. A blank customer record appears with several tabs across the top of the record:

✔ **Details:** Type the usual contact details in these fields.

Decide how you want to set up the account reference prior to beginning your data entry. Think carefully about this first data-entry field and the eight-digit short name you give each account. Sage recommends that you use an *alphanumeric* reference, meaning you use letters and numbers. Sage suggests this because you may have a number of clients with the same surname, for example, Smith, so you need to give them unique references, such as Smith01, Smith02 and so on. Alternatively, ignore any numbers and continue with just words. For example, Julian Smith is SmithJ, Sarah Smith becomes SmithS and so on.

After typing in the account reference, you can tab through the other fields and enter the relevant information.

✔ **Defaults:** The basic defaults are shown in each record, and you can override the details for each individual record if desired. You can specifically tailor the defaults for your customers as well.

✔ **Credit Control:** You can enter your credit control details here for both customers and suppliers. For example, you can set credit limits, note credit reviews and set up settlement discounts.

To avoid a nervous breakdown, tick the Terms Agreed box in the bottom left corner of the Credit Control screen. If you don't, every time you open that record, you get an audio and visual prompt saying that terms haven't been agreed with this account. You'll go crazy after a very short space of time! So if you do nothing else with this page, make sure that you tick the Terms Agreed box.

✔ **Sales/Purchases (customer/supplier record):** You can view a history of all invoices, credit notes, balances, receipts and payments against this account.

✔ **Orders:** You can see the history of all sales orders applied to this account. Double-click any of the orders to enter the detail of the sales order record. You can also create a new sales invoice or a new order from this screen.

✔ **Projects:** You can view a list of all the projects associated with this customer. You can also create a new project record for this selected customer by clicking New Project Record. (See Chapter 13 for more details.)

✔ **Graphs:** Prepare to be wowed with a graphical representation of the history of the transactions month by month.

✔ **Activity:** I use this screen a lot. It shows a list of every transaction ever made on the selected account. You can see all the invoices and credit notes, payments and receipts. It also shows a balance, amounts paid or received and turnover for that account.

✔ **Bank:** You can enter bank details on each record. This option is useful if you do a lot of online banking, particularly payment of suppliers.

✔ **Communications:** You can record details of telephone conversations with both customers and suppliers. For example, if you're making a credit control call, you can make notes of promised payments and follow-up dates for call backs, which creates an event in your Sage Diary. This information also appears in the Task Manager.

✔ **Memo:** You can attach electronic documents and files for all your customer and supplier records, using the Document Manager function.

Setting customer and supplier defaults

You can set your customer and supplier defaults by clicking on Settings from the main toolbar, and then choosing Customer or Supplier defaults. For example, in Customer defaults, you have the ability to edit the VAT code, nominal code or discounts. You can also choose whether your invoices are calendar aged or period aged. Check out the Sage Help button for more information.

Deleting customer and supplier records

You can delete a record only if there are no transactions on the account and the account balance is zero. If neither condition is met and you try to delete an account, Sage lets you know in no uncertain terms that you can't do it! But if you can, and if you must, then open the record you wish to delete and click on the Delete button.

Creating Your Nominal Records

Nominal records are the main body of an accounting system. They are categorised into a Chart of Accounts structure, which I explain in Chapter 2.

Exploring your nominal records

To explore your nominal records, click Company to open up the Nominal Ledger screen. You can change the way the information is presented on the Nominal Ledger screen by using the dropdown arrow next to the Layout field. Figure 3-1 shows the Analyser layout.

The main body of the screen shows the categories of the nominal codes. To see which codes lie within the categories, click the plus sign (+) next to each category. Doing so drills down to the next level and shows the subcategories. You can click the plus sign next to a subcategory to see the actual codes that form part of that subcategory.

Figure 3-1: Looking at the nominal ledger through the Analyser layout.

Alternatively, you can view all the nominal codes at a glance by clicking on the Layout dropdown menu at the top right corner of the screen and selecting List. The screen changes its appearance and shows a list of all your nominal codes along with a description/name. After you have transactions entered, you also see Debit and Credit columns with figures in, next to each nominal code.

You can choose the *Graph* layout, which shows a pie chart layout of the nine categories of accounts within the nominal ledger. This option is colourful, but not particularly useful. My preferred option is the List layout, which shows the nominal codes in their clearest format.

Renaming existing nominal records

You may want to rename some of your nominal records. For example, Sage helpfully gives you several Sales Type codes from *A* through *E* – meaningless descriptions that you need to change to suit your business.

For example, Jeanette, the owner of Jingles, wants to change nominal code 4000, currently designated as Sales Type A, to Sale of Greeting Cards.

This is very easily done, by opening up the record you wish
to rename, placing your cursor in the Name box, deleting the
current name and replacing it with the name of your new sales
type. For Jingles, Jeanette replaces Sales Type A with Sales of
Greeting Cards. You then simply save the record and Close.

Adding a new nominal record

When you're adding a new nominal record, you need to make
sure that the nominal code you use fits into the correct part
of the Chart of Accounts. Refer to Chapter 2 to see the nine
different ranges of nominal codes that make up the Chart of
Accounts.

If you're adding new codes into your range, you need to
decide where you can slot them into your existing structure.
For example, if you want to add a nominal record (which
requires a new nominal code) for mobile phones, look at the
Profit and Loss account, because it's an expense item. It's
not a direct product cost, so place it in the Overhead section,
close to the telephone costs for the business, around the 7500
range of nominal codes.

In the Jingles example, Jeanette wants to add a new Sales nominal record, Sale of Balloons, with a new nominal code, 4010.

Here's how to add a new nominal record:

1. **Click Company.**

2. **On the Nominal Ledger toolbar, click the Record
   icon.**

3. **In the N/C box, type the new nominal code number
   and then tab to the Name field.**

   The new nominal code for Jingles is 4010.

   The words new account pop up next to the nominal
   code because Sage doesn't recognise this nominal
   code; it isn't part of the default list of nominal codes.

4. **In the Name field, type the name of your new record.**

   For Jingles, Jeanette enters Sale of Balloons.

5. **Click Save and close the box.**

You need to check that your Chart of Accounts is free of errors; refer to Chapter 2 for instructions on how to do this.

Looking for a nominal record

Each nominal record has its own nominal code, but not every nominal code is immediately easy to find. Not that Sage tries to make things difficult, but an awful lot of codes need slotting into categories. Some codes sit into categories better than others.

Because I know a lot of the nominal codes by heart, I know where to start looking, but as a beginner you need to have some tricks up your sleeve to find those elusive codes!

Searching for a record alphabetically

If you know the name of the record you're trying to find, but not the number (nominal code), follow these steps:

1. **Click Company and then Record.**

2. **From the N/C (nominal code) field, click the right dropdown arrow.**

   A list of all your nominal codes appears, in number order.

3. **Click the grey heading Name to reorganise the nominal codes into alphabetical order. Press the appropriate letter and locate the code you're interested in.**

Finding a record numerically

If you know the approximate nominal code range, 7500, for example, but you don't know the specific code to use, click the grey heading above the numbers to re-sort in numerical order.

Looking around a nominal record

Sage provides a number of different ways to view the information contained within a nominal record. Sage also provides you with some demonstration data, and I sometimes find it helpful to explore parts of the system with dummy data already entered.

You can view the demonstration data by clicking File from
the main toolbar, then Open and Open Demo Data. Click Yes
on the confirmation window that appears. The Logon window
appears next – enter **Manager** as the Logon and leave the
password field blank. Click OK, and the demonstration data
will appear.

To access a nominal record, click Company and then Record.
Type a code in the Nominal Code field and press Enter.

To follow this example, type **4000** to bring up the Sales North
nominal record, which is shown in Figure 3-2.

Figure 3-2: Looking at a nominal record with Sage's demonstration data.

Notice the four tabs at the top of the nominal record:

- ✔ **Details:** You are already in the Details screen. This
  screen shows you actual amounts posted to this account
  on a month-by-month basis and prior-year figures if
  they're available. You can see a column for budget figures. You can edit the Budget field and enter figures
  directly into each month for each nominal record as part
  of your budget-setting process.

- ✔ **Graphs:** You can view a graphic format of the account
  information with lots of pretty colours!

✔ **Activity:** One of the most well-used screens! You can scroll up and down the screen to see exactly what transactions have been posted using this nominal code. Any credit notes or journals also show here.

As 4000 is a sales code, you can see exactly which invoices have been posted.

✔ **Memo:** You can make notes that relate to this account. Or, you can attach electronic documents with the Document Manager.

Deleting a nominal code

You can delete nominal codes that you never use, to tidy the list. For example, if you sell just one product, you may want to delete the codes associated with Sales Types B, C, D and E. You can do this by opening up the Nominal record that you want to delete and clicking on the Delete button.

You can only delete a nominal record if there are no transactions associated with that code.

Recording Your Bank Accounts

Sage automatically gives you seven bank accounts (Chapter 8 tells you more about these) that range from an Ordinary Bank Current Account to a Credit Card Receipt account. You need to review the list of bank accounts and rename some, add new ones or delete those that don't apply to your business. The following sections tell you how to do these tasks.

Renaming an existing account

You may find that the number of bank accounts that Sage gives you is sufficient, but you probably need to rename them to suit your business. For example, you may want to specify the name of the bank or type of account, such as number one account, number two account and so on. . . .

Don't create a new account if you can simply rename an existing one. You then don't need to amend your Chart of Accounts for new nominal codes.

To rename an account, simply click on the Bank and then Record icons. You can use the dropdown arrow to select the account you want to rename and then overtype the new name in the Nominal Name field. Lastly, click Save.

Creating new accounts

If you have a lot of bank accounts, you may need to create additional bank account records to accommodate your business needs. You can choose from three ways of creating a new account. You can:

- ✔ Set up a new account by using the wizard. Simply click Bank on the navigation bar and then New Account from the Task pane or the New icon from the Bank Account Module toolbar.

- ✔ Duplicate an existing account. From the Bank module, highlight the account you want to duplicate and click the Duplicate button at the bottom of the screen. Give the account an appropriate nominal code and name, click Save and off you go.

- ✔ Use a blank record and follow the steps I give here.

I demonstrate how to create a bank record with the same method used for creating customer, supplier and nominal records so far. The steps are:

1. **From the Bank module, click Record.**

   A bank record appears, with the account reference as 1200, which is the default nominal code for the Bank Current account.

2. **Click the dropdown arrow in the Account Reference box.**

   All the existing bank accounts and their nominal codes are listed.

3. **Decide on a new nominal code reference for your new bank account and enter it in the Account Reference field.**

   Try to keep all the current accounts and deposit accounts between 1200 and 1229 and credit card accounts between 1240 and 1249. The Chart of Accounts is more presentable that way.

4. **Tab down to the Nominal Name field and give your new account a name.**

5. **From the Account Type box, use the dropdown arrow to select cash, cheque or credit card account.**

6. **Skip the Balance box – don't enter anything.**

   Have a look at Chapter 4 for information on opening balances.

7. **If you're operating foreign currency accounts, select a currency.**

8. **Check *No bank reconciliation* if you're not intending to reconcile this bank account.**

   You'll probably only choose this option for the Petty Cash account. You need to reconcile all accounts, including credit card accounts, to a bank or credit card statement to get a good picture of how your business is doing.

9. **Click Save.**

Deleting a bank record

You may find that you want to delete a bank record. For example, Sage provides you with a Building Society account, which you may not want. Although you may decide to rename this account, you can choose to delete the account completely and tidy up your bank account list. However, you can only do this if the following conditions apply:

✔ The bank account has no transactions associated with it.

✔ The balance is zero.

✔ It is not a control account.

If the account meets these conditions, highlight the bank account concerned and click Delete. You receive an affirmation message. Click Yes to continue or No to return to your original record.

Getting a handle on control accounts

Sage uses control accounts to make double-entry postings. The Debtors and Creditors control accounts enable you to see total figures for all your debtors and creditors without having to add up all the individual invoices and credit notes.

To see a list of all the control accounts, click Company and then Control Accounts on the Links list. You don't need to alter these accounts because they're default accounts. In fact, if the Debtors, Creditors and Sales Tax or Purchase Tax control accounts have balances on them, you can't make any changes to these codes. Only journal to them if you're confident with your double-entry bookkeeping. Otherwise, leave them to your accountant!

Getting Your Product Records in Order

Planning your nominal codes is important, but planning your product records is just as important. The product records that you create eventually become your product list – a list of all your stock items. As the business grows, the number of stock items grows, so you need to design a stock-coding system that's easy to use and can easily identify products. You need to be able to identify a product type quickly and easily from a stock list or stock report.

Creating a product record

You can create a product record three ways:

- ✔ Use the wizard: click Products and then New.

- ✔ Duplicate an existing record: click the product and then Duplicate.

- ✔ Type your details directly into a blank product record, as detailed here. Follow these steps to use the blank record method:

1. **From the Products module, click Record.**

   The Details screen, shown in Figure 3-3, appears.

Figure 3-3: Viewing a blank product record.

2. **Enter your chosen product code, using 30 digits or fewer.**

3. **Type in a description of the product and fill in as much of the product details as you can.**

   The product field now allows you to enter the bar code for your product, alpha-numerically and up to 60 characters in length.

   In the default section, you may need to change the default sales nominal code and purchase nominal code. For example, a stock record for birthday cards requires a nominal code for birthday cards. You need to check the nominal codes and change if necessary.

   When entering your product details, you can choose an Item Type:

   - **Stock Item:** A regular item of stock, which has a product code and description. You can give a stock item a project code and issue it to a project.

   - **Non-Stock Item:** An item that isn't a usual item of stock, perhaps purchased for use within the business instead of to sell. Non-stock items can't be posted to a project as they aren't classified as stock and can't be issued.

- **Service Item:** Usually a charge, for example, a labour charge, that can be set up as a product code. Service items can't be posted to a project as they aren't physical products in stock and can't be issued.

4. **When you've finished entering your product details, click Save.**

   Your first record is saved, and the screen goes blank again, waiting for your next record.

The other tabs that belong to the product record are outlined next. You may need to enter details in the BOM tab if you're using Bill of Materials. (See Chapter 12 for more details on this.) Other tabs can just be used as monitoring tools, such as product activity or sales.

- ✔ **Memo:** You can attach electronic documents to the product record or enter additional notes about the product.

- ✔ **BOM (Bill of Materials):** BOM is where you can create a product from an amalgamation of other products that you may have in stock. BOM is a list of products and components required to make up the main product.

- ✔ **Sales:** This tab shows you the sales value and quantity sold month by month for that product. The Actuals column is driven from actual invoices raised. You can enter budget values and prior-year information for each month. This information allows you to produce useful comparison reports for that product.

- ✔ **Graph:** You can see a graphical representation of products sold against budget and the prior year at a glance.

- ✔ **Activity:** Shows the individual transactions created for each product. For example, goods in, out, transferred or stock adjustments. You can also view the quantity of the item in stock, on order, allocated and available.

- ✔ **Discount:** Allows you to give up to five different quantity discounts per product.

- ✔ **Web:** You can enter information about your web shop, including images of your product.

Editing a product record

You can edit a product record at any time by double-clicking the chosen product. The Product Record screen appears. You can then make the necessary change, click Save and close the screen.

Deleting a product record

As with the other records, you can only delete a product record if the following criteria are met:

- ✔ The product record has no transactions on the product activity. Any history needs to be removed; see Chapter 15 for information on how to do this.

- ✔ The In Stock, On Order and Allocated balances are all zero.

- ✔ The product is not a component of a Bill of Materials.

- ✔ The product has no outstanding transactions, such as outstanding orders.

If all these conditions are met, you can delete the product by opening up the product record and clicking on the Delete button at the bottom of the record.

Entering a project record

You can create a project record in one of the following ways:

- ✔ Summon the Project Record wizard in one of two ways: from the Projects module, click the New icon; or select New Project from the Task pane.

- ✔ From the Customer Record window, click New Project.

- ✔ Enter details directly into a blank project record, which I describe next.

- ✔ When you create a sales order with the product code S3, you have the option to create a project for that order.

To enter project details from a blank record, click Record from the Project module. The project record opens on the Details tab and gives you access to other relevant tabs:

- ✔ **Details tab:** Enter your project details, including start dates, completion dates and contact names and addresses here. You must have a unique project reference before you can save the project. If you need to, you can link a project directly to a customer by clicking on the A/C Ref field in the Customer Details section and selecting your customer using the dropdown arrow. If the project is internal, leave this blank (in other words, don't select a customer).

- ✔ **Analysis tab:** You can enter the price quoted for a project on this screen. All the other information falls into the look-but-don't-touch category – you can see it, but you can't change it. As you create and post invoices to raise bills to your customer for the project, the billing total is updated. You also have an analysis of the total budget and costs associated with this project.

- ✔ **Activity tab:** You can view the transactions posted against a project here – invoices, costs and product movements, for example.

- ✔ **Budgets and Structure tabs:** The Budgets tab records monies allocated to the project. The Structure tab is used to maintain a project that has several phases; both are applied to the project record after it has been created. As the project is being created, you apply all costs associated with it.

- ✔ **Memo tab:** Using the Attachments pane, you can add electronic documents or filing references to each project. You can edit the memo pad as you require.

After you enter the project details, click Save, and your new project appears in the Projects screen.

Setting Up Fixed Asset Records

Fixed assets are items usually held in the business for at least 12 months or more. When the business purchases a fixed asset, such as a building, a vehicle or machinery, instead of deducting the whole expense at the time of purchase, the asset is *depreciated* over the extent of its useful life. (Sorry, I'm going into accountant-speak here.) Basically, the charge to your Profit and Loss account is apportioned over a longer period of time. For example, you may apportion the cost of a car over a four-year period instead of charging the whole cost in the first year.

To keep track of your depreciated items, you need to set up a fixed asset record, so that Sage knows what items are fixed assets, and over what period and at what rate they need to be depreciated. To set up a fixed asset record, follow these steps:

1. **Click Company and then select Manage Fixed Assets from the Task pane.**

   To begin with, the main screen is blank. As you start to record your assets, the screen fills up with detail, one line per asset.

2. **Click Record. Use the Details tab to describe the asset and give it a reference.**

   Enter information as necessary on the Posting tab, as shown in Figure 3-4 and detailed here:

Figure 3-4: Entering information onto a fixed asset record.

- Select a Department if required.

- Use the Balance Sheet Depreciation N/C drop-down arrow to select the appropriate code. Remember, this record requires a Balance Sheet code, so it starts with 00. For example, Plant and Machinery Depreciation is 0021.

- Use the Profit and Loss Depreciation dropdown arrow to select your code. Now you need a Profit and Loss code, so take care to select the correct one. For example, Plant and Machinery depreciation is 8001.

You may feel confused by the two codes for depreciation – one in the Balance Sheet and one in the Profit and Loss account – but remember that Sage operates a double-entry bookkeeping system and needs two codes to post your transactions to. Just be careful when setting up your codes to select the correct ones.

- Select the Depreciation Method, usually straight line or reducing balance. If you're not sure, check with your accountant.

- Set the Depreciation Rate. The depreciation rate is the percentage rate that reduces the value of the asset.

- Enter the cost price, net of VAT of the asset.

3. **Enter the current book value of the item you're depreciating.**

   If the item is brand new, the book value is the same as cost price. If the item has already been depreciated, the book value is cost price less depreciation. If you decide to use the reducing balance method, the book value is the value used to calculate the depreciation amount. Sage automatically updates the remaining boxes.

4. **Click Save when you're happy with the information you've entered.**

Sage posts depreciation when you run the Month-End option. For more details, go to Chapter 15. If you have to delete an asset – because you sold it or it was stolen or damaged – follow these steps:

1. **Click Company and then Manage Fixed Assets (from the Links list).**

2. **Select the asset and click Delete.**

3. **Click Yes to agree to the confirmation message or No to return to the previous menu.**

Chapter 4

Recording Your Opening Balances

∙ ∙

In This Chapter

▶ Choosing the right time to switch to Sage

▶ Getting your opening balances

▶ Recording your opening balances

▶ Checking for accuracy

∙ ∙

*I*n this chapter I explain how to transfer the individual account balances from your previous accounting system, whether it is manual or computerised, into Sage 50 Accounts. Effectively, you're taking the values that make up what your business is worth on the day you swap from your old system and start using Sage. You need to set up your nominal records before recording balances, so check out Chapter 3 if you haven't done that yet.

Opening balances give you a true picture of your business's assets and liabilities to use as a starting point. If you don't enter your opening balances, you don't have accurate information about who owes you money, how much money you owe or how much money you have in the bank. You won't even be able to reconcile your bank balance. In short, without opening balances, the information in your Sage program isn't worth the paper it's printed on!

Entering your opening balances can be a bit tricky, so make sure that you're not going to be disturbed too much! After you've done this, you can print an opening balance sheet, which is an important tool to check that your balances have been entered correctly.

Timing Your Switch to Sage

The best time to start with a new system is at the beginning of a financial year. You roll the closing balances from the previous year-end forward so that they become your opening balances for your new year. Take advice from your accountant if you have one, as everyone's circumstances are different.

If you can't wait until the new financial year to switch to Sage and you're VAT registered, at least wait until the start of a new VAT quarter. This way, you avoid having a mixture of transactions in your old and new system, which makes reconciling your data extremely difficult.

Enter your opening balances before you start entering transactions. You can then check your accuracy by proving your opening Trial Balance matches your Closing Trial Balance from your previous system. Without the clutter of day-to-day transactions you can check much more easily!

Obtaining Your Opening Balances

Whether you're transferring from a manual bookkeeping system or a computerised one, the process is still the same. Essentially, you transfer into Sage the balance sheet information that shows the net worth of your business.

An opening *Trial Balance* is a list of all account balances carried forward from the previous year-end. Your previous accounting system is your source for your Trial Balance. As you zero-down your Profit and Loss items at the end of the financial year, any retained Profit and Loss items from the previous year now sit in your balance sheet, so an opening Trial Balance contains only balance sheet codes. An opening Trial Balance report looks quite short and shows debit and credit entries for all your balance sheet items, with grand totals at the bottom of both your Debit and Credit columns.

If you're starting to use Sage at the beginning of a new financial year, your accountant can provide you with your opening balances.

If you're transferring from a manual bookkeeping system, you need to ensure that you've balanced off all your individual accounts for the previous period. You may find it easier to print off a list of your newly created nominal accounts in Sage and create two columns, one for debit balances, and the other for credit balances. (To print a nominal list, click Company, which takes you to the Nominal Ledger screen, and then click Print List.) You can then total each column to create an opening Trial Balance.

The figures contained within a Trial Balance are simply the accumulated value of items. For example, the Debtors control account is simply the combined value of all monies owed by customers at that point in time. To establish your opening balances, you need to know the specifics of exactly which customers owe you money and what invoices are outstanding. The same applies to your suppliers: you need to see a full breakdown of who you owe money to. You obtain this information from a variety of sources. Table 4-1 shows the types of reports you need from a computerised system or a manual one.

Table 4-1   Information Sources for Entering Opening Balances

Category	Computerised System	Manual System
Customers		
For a standard VAT system, record the transaction including VAT. For a VAT cash accounting scheme, record both the net and VAT amount. If this figure isn't the same as your opening Debtors Balance, you need to investigate why.	An Aged Debtors report, showing a breakdown of who owed you money at the start of the year/period.	A list of customers who haven't paid at the year-end, including the amount outstanding.

(continued)

Table 4-1 *(continued)*

Category	Computerised System	Manual System
Suppliers		
For a standard VAT scheme, include the VAT amount. For a VAT cash account-ing scheme, show both the net and VAT amount. If this figure isn't the same as your opening Creditors Balance, you need to investigate why.	An Aged Creditors report, showing a breakdown of who you owed money to at the start of the year/period.	A list of suppliers who you haven't paid at the year-end, along with the monies owed.
Bank		
When you start reconciling the first month's bank account you may see cheques from the prior year clearing through the bank account. You don't need to worry about these unpre-sented cheques and lodgements as they've already been taken into account in the previous year and are included in the open-ing balance for your bank account. Simply mark the items on your bank statement as being prior-year entries. Don't post the items through again.	A copy of the bank statements showing the balance at the year-end. A copy of the bank reconcili-ation showing a list of any unpresented cheques or outstand-ing deposits. (Your accountant can help with this.)	A copy of the bank statements showing the balance at the year-end. A copy of the bank reconcili-ation showing a list of any unpresented cheques or outstand-ing deposits. (Your accountant can help with this.)
Products		
	A stocktake list show-ing the number of items in stock at the start of the year/period.	A stocktake list show-ing the number of items in stock at the start of the year/period.

Entering Opening Balances

The opening balances represent the financial position of your business on the day you start entering transactions into Sage. Even a new business has opening balances as the funds used to start it up need to be accounted for – the owner's money or grant funding, for example.

Work through your opening Trial Balance systematically and tick off each balance as you enter it into Sage. At the end of this process you can print an opening Trial Balance from Sage that replicates the one from your previous accounting system – in theory at least!

Entering customer and supplier balances

Despite the fact that customers owe you money and you owe money to suppliers, the process for entering opening balances for both is pretty much the same, so I talk about them together in this section.

If you used wizards to create your customer and supplier records, you've already entered your opening balances because the wizard asks for them.

I use the Record icon as opposed to the wizard option when setting up records (as I explain in Chapter 3). Using this method,

1. **Select the account using the dropdown arrow and click the OB (Opening Balance) button located to the right of the Balance box (see Figure 4-1).**

   The Opening Balance Set-up window appears.

Ref	Date	Type	Gross
	26/11/2010	Invoice	0.00

Save   Cancel

Figure 4-1: The Opening Balance Set-up window.

2. **Click the Reference field and type** opening balance.

3. **Tab to the date field and enter the original date of the invoice/credit note.**

4. **Select whether the entry is an invoice or credit note.**

5. **Enter the amount.**

6. **Record the gross amount including VAT for standard VAT accounting users; record the net amount and VAT separately if using the VAT cash accounting scheme.**

7. **Continue using a separate line for each invoice.**

8. **Click Save when you've finished.**

9. **Check that your customer balance agrees with your Aged Debtors or customer list for customers, and your Aged Creditors or supplier list for suppliers.**

You have the options of entering a zero balance (which is appropriate if you haven't yet dealt with a new customer or supplier), one lump sum figure or individual transactions. I recommend entering each transaction so that you can see at a glance on the Activity record exactly which invoices make up the opening balance. I strongly urge you to avoid entering a lump sum – it's not best practice and can cause you problems later on.

Recording opening bank balances

You need to record the opening balance for each bank account associated with your business.

Only post opening balances by using nominal journals (see Chapter 15 for information about nominal journals) if you're confident using double-entry bookkeeping. To avoid complications, I recommend that you use the Opening Balance button in each individual bank record in the same way as when entering customer and supplier opening balances.

You may have uncleared payments or receipts already included in your bank balance shown on the opening Trial Balance. The best way to deal with uncleared payments is to obtain a copy of your bank reconciliation statement at the year-end and identify those items shown as unpresented cheques or outstanding paid-in items. After your bank statement arrives, mark these items on your statement as being pre-year-end transactions. When you come to reconcile your bank account in Sage, you can ignore these items as they're already included in your opening balances.

You can enter your opening bank balances from your record icon within the bank module. When you enter the account balance, if the account is in the black, enter the account balance in the Receipt box. If the account is overdrawn, put the amount in the Payment box. You can click Save when you're happy that the opening balance figure is correct.

Recording nominal opening balances

If you use the opening Trial Balance or list of account balances as your checking document, or if you followed the order of this chapter, you've already entered the Debtors control account, the Creditors control account and the opening bank balances, so you don't want to enter them again.

When you enter the individual opening balances on to each customer record, Sage does some double-entry in the background, crediting the Sales account and debiting the Debtors control account; therefore when you come to enter the remaining nominal account balances from your Trial Balance, don't post the Debtors control account total, otherwise you are double-counting. If you do post the Debtors control account balance in error, you need to reverse the posting by using a nominal journal. Turn to Chapter 15 for information on journals.

Working in a methodical manner, enter all the remaining balances, such as fixed assets, stock, loans and so on, using the following steps:

1. **From Company, click Record.**

2. **Enter the nominal code.**

   If you're using the Sage default set of nominal codes, use common sense and match the items from your opening Trial Balance to those of Sage. For example, Accruals in Sage has the nominal code 2109. Take the balance for Accruals from your opening Trial Balance and use nominal code 2109.

3. **Click the OB button next to the Balance box.**

    The Opening Balance Set-up window appears.

4. **Keep the reference (Ref) as O/Bal (opening balance) and tab along to the Date field and enter the closing date of the prior period.**

5. **Tab to the Debit or Credit column and enter a debit or credit figure from the opening Trial Balance.**

6. **Click Save.**

You must use the prior year-end date as your opening balance date so that the Trial Balance you bring forward is correct. If you inadvertently enter 1 April as your date, the figure you enter drops into the current year and not into the brought-forward category. To rectify this, enter a nominal journal to reverse the previous journal that Sage automatically posted for you. (See Chapter 15 for help.) If you want to view the automatic journal that Sage has posted, click Company from the navigation bar and then click Financials from the Links list.

Putting in opening balances for products

You only need to do this if you want to track stock items.

Make sure that you create product records for all the items of stock that you wish to put an opening balance to before you try to enter opening product balances. (Refer to Chapter 3 for information on creating records.)

Use the Record icon as in preceding sections and enter the opening stock figure. Check outthe example in Figure 4-2 where Jeanette, the owner of a fictional card company, has created a record with the product code Card-HB for birthday cards. Her stocktake at the year-end showed 1,000 cards in stock.

Figure 4-2: Registering a thousand birthday cards.

After you click Save, Sage posts an Adjustment In (AI) transaction to the product record, which you can see in the Activity tab. To view activity on an item, from the main screen click the stock item you want to view and double-click the product to take you into the record. Click the Activity tab to see the adjustment posting.

The product opening figures don't automatically update a stock value into your nominal ledger. Opening stock is one of the figures you enter as part of your nominal ledger opening balances – see the 'Recording nominal opening balances' section earlier in this chapter.

Checking Your Opening Balances

Make sure that the figures you entered are correct and agree with the opening Trial Balance you used to enter those figures. The best way to do this is to print your own opening Trial Balance from Sage and compare it to the document you've been working with. If you find discrepancies, you can go back and fix them.

Printing an opening Trial Balance

Follow these instructions to run an opening Trial Balance:

1. **From the navigation bar, click Company and then click Financials in the Links list.**

2. **From Financials, click the Trial icon at the top of the page.**

3. **Select Preview and Run in the Print Output box.**

4. **Change the date in the Criteria Values box to Brought Forward, using the dropdown arrow.**

5. **Click OK.**

   This previews the opening Trial Balance.

6. **Click the Print icon to print the Trial Balance and check your report.**

Look for the following information on the report:

   ✔ Check that the *suspense account* (the temporary account
     where you put problematic transactions until you deter-
     mine where they properly belong) shows a zero balance.

   ✔ Check that the totals on your new Trial Balance are the
     same as the totals on the Trial Balance from your previ-
     ous system.

If you have problems with either of these balances, see the
next section.

Dealing with errors

If the suspense account doesn't have a zero balance, first
check that you haven't entered the Debtors or Creditors control account twice. If you've entered something twice, turn to
Chapter 15, which tells you how to reverse out the duplicated
item using a nominal journal.

If you find that your total balance doesn't match the total of
your opening Trial Balance, make sure that you've entered an
opening balance for each nominal code and that you haven't
missed anything out by mistake.

After you enter all your opening balances and your opening
Trial Balance matches that of your previous system, you're
now in a position to begin entering your transactions, so turn
to the next chapter!

Part II
Looking into Day-to-Day Functions

'There – we've got to stop storing petty cash in a tin and use a computerised petty cash system.'

Part II

Day Transactions

In this part . . .

I look at the day-to-day functionality of the system, taking you through issuing sales invoices, entering purchase invoices and doing banking transactions. I show you how to maintain and correct your transactions, which hopefully leads to correct information and good reporting!

Chapter 5

Processing Your Customer Paperwork

*I*n this chapter I tell you how to process the sales invoices for your company. If you want to process invoices created manually or from another system, such as Word, this is the chapter for you! Alternatively, if you prefer to produce your sales invoices directly from Sage, check out Chapter 6.

Posting Batch Entry Invoices

Don't you just groan when you see a huge pile of invoices that need entering? Well, Sage can help you speed your way through them by allowing you to post batches of invoices. In other words, you can enter several invoices on the same screen and post them all at the same time as a batch onto the system. (*Post* is a way to say *enter information into an account.*)

Use this method to record sales invoices raised from a system other than Sage. For example, you can issue invoices with Microsoft Word and then enter the invoices onto Sage by using batch entry.

You can enter any number of invoices in one sitting. For example, if you have 20 invoices to process for the day, you can enter them all onto one screen and then check the total of that batch to ensure accuracy. Larger companies often process large quantities of invoices in a number of smaller batches, which makes processing a more manageable task.

You can enter one invoice per line on your Batch Entry screen, but remember that if you have an invoice where the value needs to be split into two different nominal codes, you need to use two lines for that one invoice.

When you have a batch of invoices in front of you, follow these steps:

1. **Click Customer and then click the Invoice icon.**

   The Batch Customer Invoices screen appears.

2. **Click the A/C (Account) field and use the dropdown arrow to select the correct customer account for the invoice.**

3. **Enter the invoice date.**

   Sage automatically enters the system date, which is usually the current day's date. Make sure that you change this date to the one on the invoice.

4. **Enter the invoice number in the Ref (Reference) field.**

   Every invoice needs a unique number derived from a sequential system.

5. **Add any additional references in the Ex Ref field.**

   You can choose to leave this field blank or enter order numbers or other references.

6. **Change the nominal code, if necessary, in the N/C (Nominal Code) field.**

   This field automatically defaults to 4000, unless you changed the nominal default code on the Default tab of your customer record.

7. **Click the department (Dept) applicable for your invoice.**

   You can leave this field blank if you don't have any departments set up. If, on the other hand, you want to be able to analyse information from different offices or divisions within the company, setting up departments is the way to go:

- From the navigation bar, click Company.
- Click Department from the Links list.

    You can then enter departments as you wish, using the New/Edit icon.

8. **If you're using projects, click the dropdown Project Ref arrow to select the appropriate project.**

    You can leave this field blank if you don't use projects.

9. **Describe what the invoice is for in the Details field.**

10. **Enter the amount net of VAT in the Net field.**

11. **Choose the tax code applicable for this invoice in the T/C (Tax Code) field.**

    Some common VAT codes:

    - T0: Zero-rated transactions.
    - T1: Standard rate 20 per cent.
    - T2: Exempt transactions.
    - T4: Sales to VAT-registered customers in the European Community (EC).
    - T5: Lower VAT rate at 5 per cent.
    - T7: Zero-rated purchases from suppliers in the EC.
    - T8: Standard-rated purchases from suppliers in the EC.
    - T9: Transactions not involving VAT, for example journal entries.

    The system updates the VAT field according to the tax code you choose.

Make sure that the VAT Sage calculates is the same as the amount on the invoice. Sometimes Sage rounds up the VAT, and you may find you have a penny difference. If that happens, overwrite the VAT amount in Sage so that the amounts match.

12. **Perform a quick check of the total value of the invoices you're about to post.**

   To do this:

   - Add up the gross value of the pile of invoices you've just entered.

   - Check this total against the total on your Batch Entry screen (in the top right corner of your Sage screen).

   If the totals are different, check each line on your Batch Entry screen against the invoices.

13. **Click Save when the totals in Step 12 are the same.**

 To speed up the entry of invoices, you can use the function keys. To see how the F6, F7 and F8 keys can help you, have a quick look at Chapter 18.

Creating Credit Notes

A *credit note* is the opposite of an invoice. Instead of charging the customer, as you do with an invoice, you refund money to a customer through a credit note. Posting a credit note reverses or cancels an invoice you entered previously.

You use credit notes for a number of different reasons. Invoices may need to be cancelled because the product sent was wrong, the goods have been returned and so on.

 To ensure that you raise the credit note correctly, you must identify which invoice you're trying to correct. You need to know the invoice number, the date it was raised and the nominal code it was posted to. It's important that you use the same nominal code on your credit note as you used on your invoice. This way, the double-entry bookkeeping posts the entries in the correct nominal codes, so you don't find odd balances showing in the accounts!

You can produce credit notes from the Invoicing module I describe in Chapter 6, but if you're not invoicing directly from Sage, you must use the batch-entry method for processing them. The process is exactly the same as for invoices, so jump back to Chapter 6 to see how it's done. Just be aware that the font colour changes from black to red when you're entering credit note information. This feature is useful, as the Credit Note screen looks identical to the Invoice screen. You wouldn't be the first person to merrily continue entering credit notes rather than invoices!

Use the Details field to record the specifics of the credit note. For example, put something like 'Credit note against Invoice No. 123', and if possible add a description as to why the credit is necessary – the goods were faulty, for example.

Registering Payments from Your Customers

Whenever you're dealing with money, whether a payment to a supplier, a cheque from a customer or any other kind of money transaction, use the Bank module. Don't forget this as you process your transactions!

The Bank module has several icons across the top. Use the Customer icon to post a customer receipt.

Don't go directly to the Receipt icon as the info under this icon helps you process things like bank interest received, grants received and so on – it doesn't record the money you receive from customers.

Matching payments to invoices

Ideally, when a customer sends you a cheque you also receive a *remittance advice slip.* This slip identifies which invoices the customer is paying with the cheque sent in. You then pay the cheque into the bank, using a *paying-in slip,* which is kept for your accounting records.

To match the cheque to the correct invoices, follow this procedure:

1. **From the Bank module, click Customer.**

2. **Select the account you wish to post the receipt against by using the dropdown arrow.**

As soon as you open an account, you can see all out-standing items displayed on the main body of the screen. The first column shows the transaction number and the second column displays the transaction type: *SI* marks a sales invoice; *SC* indicates a sales credit.

The top part of the Customer Receipt screen is split into three sections: the first column identifies the bank account; the second shows the customer details and the third shows the receipt details.

3. **Enter the date that the money was received in the Receipt Details column.**

   If you're recording a cheque paid into the bank, type the date from the paying-in slip.

4. **Tab past the Amount field without entering an amount.**

5. **Type BACS (for Bankers' Automated Clearing Services) in the Reference field if the invoice is being paid automatically. Or, put a paying-in slip reference if paid by cheque.**

6. **Tab to the next field.**

   Sage takes you to the Receipt column of the first line of transactions.

7. **Click the Pay in Full button at the bottom of the screen.**

   The top right box (the Amount field you ignored in Step 4) now shows the amount of the invoice paid. In the Jingles example in Figure 5-1, the amount shows £235, which is the total of the first invoice.

Figure 5-1: A customer receipt after clicking the Pay in Full button.

8. **Click Save at the lower left of the screen if you're happy that the receipt amount is correct.**

   If things aren't right, click Discard. A confirmation button appears: click Yes to continue discarding and your data is cleared ready to start again.

   After you click Save, the screen returns to the original Customer Receipt screen ready for your next customer receipt.

9. **Click Close to finish after you're done entering all your receipts.**

You need to enter and save each receipt individually.

If you want to see what's happened in your Customer account, click the Activity tab. Figure 5-2 shows the Activity tab for Jingles' customer, the Village Shop. The sales receipt is showing on the account. However, two unallocated items still remain on this account. In the next section, I show you how to allocate credit notes to invoices, rather than payments to invoices.

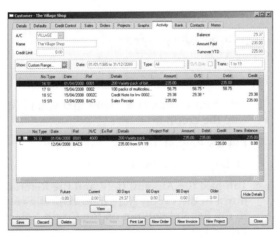

Figure 5-2: The Activity tab for the Village Shop.

Giving credit where due – allocating credit notes

As well as knowing how to allocate a payment specifically to an invoice, you also need to know how to allocate a credit note against an invoice. Because a credit note is usually raised to cancel the whole or part of an invoice, it stands to reason that the two are matched off against one another.

Allocating means matching a specific invoice to a specific payment or credit note.

Referring back to Figure 5-2, you can see that two of the entries each have an asterisk against them. The asterisk means that the item is unallocated or unmatched. The two unallocated items are sales invoice number 0002 and the credit note 00002C. You can tell that they should be allocated against each other because the description on the credit note refers to invoice 0002. However, the value of the credit note doesn't exactly equal the invoice, so you need to be careful, as you can't match the two items by using the Pay in Full button.

The steps to allocating a credit note are almost identical to allocating a customer receipt:

1. **From the Bank module, click Customer.**

2. **Select the customer account that you need to allocate the credit note to.**

3. **Put the date of the credit note in the Date field.**

   In the example, the date is 15.04.08.

4. **Tab past the Amount field and the Reference field, down to the Credit Note line. With the cursor sitting in the Receipt column on the Credit Note line, click Pay in Full.**

   Figure 5-3 shows the Village Shop account with a –£29.38 balance in the Analysis Total field in the bottom right corner. This indicates that the credit note value is ready to allocate against the invoice.

Figure 5-3: Allocating a credit note to a customer invoice.

5. **Click the Receipt column on the line that has the invoice you wish to allocate against and manually enter the value of the credit note you're allocating.**

   The Analysis Total now reduces to zero.

6. **Click Save if you're happy that you've allocated the correct amount against the invoice.**

The Customer Activity tab for the Village Shop now shows an outstanding balance of £29.37 – the remaining part of invoice 0002. The small letter *p* against the balance indicates that it's been part paid or part allocated.

Recording payments on account

You may receive payment from a customer that you can't match to a specific invoice. For example, a customer may have inadvertently paid an invoice twice (it does happen) or have forgotten to include the remittance advice slip, so you're not sure which invoice to allocate the payment to.

You can still enter the receipt onto your customer account, but you may not be able to allocate it against a specific invoice.

To enter a payment on account, from the Bank module, click Customer and select the correct customer account. Enter the date of the receipt, simply put the amount in the amount field, and click Save. Sage will tell you there is an unallocated balance and you should confirm that this is OK. The receipt will now show as a payment on account on the system.

Deleting Invoices and Credit Notes

The traditional accounting method for reversing an invoice is to create a credit note for the same amount. However, Sage has made it even easier to sort out such problems: you can simply delete the invoice. That way, you don't have to raise the credit note or allocate it to the invoice. You maintain an audit trail, as any deleted items still show and are highlighted in red, so your accountant can always see what you've been up to!

You can use the Maintenance option to cancel unwanted transactions. See Chapter 9 for details on how to delete a transaction.

Chapter 6

Invoicing Your Customers

●　●

In This Chapter

▶ Choosing an invoice type

▶ Setting up product and service invoices

▶ Printing, updating and deleting invoices

▶ Getting familiar with time-saving features

●　●

*Y*ou can generate invoices directly from your Sage accounting software, which means that you can streamline your paperwork process by printing invoices quickly – even directly from sales orders if you're using Sage Accounts Professional. So you have more time to make more money for your business – or more time to take a break from making money for your business.

Sage is an integrated system, which means that when you produce a sales invoice, the system automatically updates the nominal ledger and the customer account, along with products and projects if you're using those options.

Deciding on an Invoice Type

Depending on the type of business you run, you issue mainly one of two types of invoices:

▸ **Product invoices:** Used for businesses that sell physical items – cards, widgets, folderols and what-have-yous. A manufacturing company issues product invoices, using product codes.

▸ **Service invoices:** Used for businesses that don't sell tangible products, but provide a service to their clients.

A business that sells physical products may need to generate a service invoice occasionally. For example Manufacturers of Widgets might service some of the products they manufacture, and the engineer's time is charged using a service invoice. However, a business that provides services rarely needs to send a product invoice. For example a consultant charges for the time spent providing a service, but usually doesn't need to issue product invoices.

If you need to send invoices with both service details and product items on the same invoice, you need to have Sage Accounts Professional; otherwise you have to send one invoice for service items and another for product items. For example, a car repair centre needs product invoices for the sale of parts and service invoices to show the labour costs for servicing vehicles.

Creating Invoices

You can create both product and service invoices in much the same way, so I combine the two methods in this section and simply highlight the differences between the two as I go along.

Before you start your product invoices, make sure that you've set up your product records, which I explain how to do in Chapter 3.

To begin creating your invoices, from the Customers Task pane, click New Invoice. The Product Invoice screen comes up, as shown in Figure 6-1. The next sections cover the four tabs on the Product Invoice screen.

Issuing a proforma invoice

A *proforma invoice* is an invoice supplied in advance of the goods or services being provided. It is a more formal and detailed version of a quote.

You can create a proforma in the same way as a sales invoice. However, after you receive payment for a proforma, you need to convert it to an actual invoice. To do this, open up the proforma and change the Type field from Proforma to Invoice using the dropdown arrow in the top right corner of the screen. You can then update the record.

Note: A proforma invoice isn't considered a valid VAT invoice and can't be used in your VAT return.

Figure 6-1: Creating a blank product invoice.

Putting in the details

The Invoice screen opens with the Details tab, where the default invoice-type is for a product invoice, as indicated in the upper-right corner of the screen.

Starting in that corner, you can set options for your invoice, including:

- ✔ **Type:** Use the dropdown arrow if you want to change from an invoice to a credit note (or proforma if you're using Professional – refer to the preceding sidebar, 'Issuing a proforma invoice').

- ✔ **Format:** You can choose product or service invoice. (In the Professional version, you can produce invoices that include both elements. The following sidebar 'Mixing product and service invoices' tells you how to do this.)

- ✔ **Date:** This automatically defaults to today's date, so change it if necessary.

- ✔ **Account:** Select your customer account, using the drop-down arrow.

- ✔ **Invoice Number:** The <Autonumber> notation here unsur-prisingly indicates that Sage automatically numbers your invoices. It starts with number 1 and then automatically increases by one for each subsequent invoice. If you want to start with a different number, from the navigation bar, click Customers, and then click Invoice/Order Defaults from the Links list and select the Options tab.

✔ **Order Number:** You can enter your own order number here or leave it blank. However, if you're using Professional and generated the invoice using Sales Order Processing, an order number automatically appears within this box.

✔ **Item Number:** This shows the item line of the invoice that the cursor is currently sitting on.

✔ **Rate:** This field appears only in Professional versions of Sage when you enable the Foreign Trader facility

Getting to the main attraction

The main body of the invoice has the most differences between product invoices and services invoices. As you would expect from a product invoice, you must select the product code, which in turn comes up with the product description and a Quantity field. A service invoice doesn't require these items; instead it has a Details field.

Producing product invoices

Enter the following fields when creating a product invoice:

✔ **Product Code:** Normally you set up product codes within product records. You can type in the relevant product code directly or use the dropdown arrow.

You may encounter instances where a regular, everyday product code isn't suitable and you need a special product code, such as:

- **M Message Line:** Use this to add extra lines of description or to make comments about the products.

- **S1 Special Product Item Tax Chargeable:** Use this for product items that are standard VAT rated and don't have their own product code.

- **S2 Special Product Item Zero Rated:** Use this code for zero-rated items that don't have their own product code.

- **S3 Special Service Items Tax Chargeable:** Use S3 when you want to add service items to product invoices and sales orders. This uses the standard VAT code.

If your S1–S3 codes don't appear in your dropdown list, using the navigation bar, click Customers and from the Links list, click Customer Invoice/Order Defaults and make sure that you tick the Show Special Product Codes invoicing box.

✔ **Description:** The product description displays automatically from the product record, but you can overwrite it if necessary. You can also click F3 to edit the item line and add any one-off product details or comments.

✔ **Quantity:** Enter the number of items you're invoicing. Sage automatically shows a *1* if a quantity is in stock or *0* if no items are in stock. If you don't have enough stock for the quantity you enter, Sage issues a warning – it's difficult (not to mention illegal!) to charge people without delivering the product, so pay attention to the warning.

✔ **Price:** The unit price for the product record appears here, but you can change this if you need to.

Mixing product and service invoices

If you're using the Professional version of Sage Accounts, you have the facility to produce invoices that include both products and service elements. To do this, start by simply raising a product invoice and then at the point you want to raise a service charge, select the S3 special product code. The Edit Item line for a service invoice opens. Follow the steps in the 'Selecting service invoices' section later in this chapter for details on how to complete this transaction.

You can process all other details, including order details and footer and payment details, in the normal manner.

You can save the invoice and print it whenever you decide. If you're not happy with the invoice contents, click Discard prior to saving to clear your entries and enable you to start again.

Although you've saved the invoice, you can still make changes and resave it.

Selecting service invoices

A service invoice has fewer columns in the main body than a product invoice.

After you enter the header details for your invoice (customer details, date and so on), you then need to add the details of the service provided.

- ✔ **Details:** You can expand the information entered in the Details field by using the F3 key. This function allows you to add additional information to the invoice detail. You can only use F3 after you've entered some information into the Details field.

- ✔ **Amount:** You can enter the amount using the Edit Item Line window that appeared if you used the F3 key in the Details field. Alternatively, if you didn't need to use the F3 key for additional details, add only one line of detail on the main screen and then tab across to the Amount column and enter the amount there.

Figure 6-2 shows what happens after the insertion of the detail Hire of Clown for Party into the Details field. As soon as you type in the description, press F3 and the edit box appears. Sage duplicates the words typed into both the Description and the Details field.

Figure 6-2: Use the F3 function key to expand the details of the service invoice.

You can now apply the number of hours the clown worked and enter the unit price. You can also check that the nominal code is one that you want to use or adjust it where necessary. In this case, you may choose to change the nominal code shown in the Jingles illustration from 4000 for Sale of Cards (the default nominal code) to a more suitable code, such as Party Organising. Because Party Organising isn't an existing code, you'd then need to create a new nominal code. Refer to Chapter 3 to see how to do this.

After you're happy with the details on the main body of the invoice, the following steps are the same for both product and service invoices:

> ✔ **Net:** This is an automatic calculation, which also applies any discount attached to this customer account. Change the discount by using the F3 key if you need to.
>
> An additional Discount and Discount Percentage column shows if you selected this option within Invoice/Order defaults. Click the Discount tab and tick the Show Discount on Main Invoice/Order box.
>
> ✔ **VAT:** Sage automatically calculates this column. You can only edit it if you selected the Item VAT Amendable box on the VAT tab of Company Preferences on the main toolbar.

Then you get to the bottom of the Invoice screen, where Sage does much of the work for you:

> ✔ **Total:** Sage totals the invoice, showing net, VAT and any carriage charges applied.
>
> ✔ **Deposit:** This new feature has a smart link – a little grey arrow that takes you to the Payment tab of the invoice if clicked, so you can record any deposits received against the invoice.
>
> Sage 50 Accounts also offers a Pay by Card option, but you have to register for Sage Payment Solutions to use it. To find out more about this, from the main toolbar, click Weblinks and select Sage Payment Solutions or click Help from the main toolbar and type in **Sage Payment Solutions**.

✔ **Deduction:** With this new feature, you have the ability to provide a net value discount on the Details tab of your invoice (see the next point). You can use this feature to offer seasonal discount promotions or one-off offers.

✔ **Net Value Discount:** Click the dropdown arrow in the Description box to reveal an Edit Item line. You can enter information referring to the discount and a discount value and then press Tab, and Sage automatically calculates the percentage discount. If you enter a discount percentage, the value is calculated for you.

Filling in the order details

You can use the Order Details tab to fill in details of where the goods are being delivered and who took the order. You can also add up to three lines of text. If the order can be left outside by the chicken shed, this is the place to share that information!

Getting down to the footer details

You can enter carriage terms, settlement terms and global details in the Footer Details tab:

✔ **Carriage terms:** You may want to assign carriage costs to the invoice. You may have postal or courier costs. You can set up specific nominal codes to charge carriage costs. If you set up departments, use the dropdown list to select the appropriate one. You can also add the consignment number and courier details and track your parcel by accessing the courier's website.

✔ **Settlement Terms:** Some information may already be present in these boxes if you entered the details on the customer record. You can enter the number of days during which an early settlement discount applies, if any. You can see what discount percentage is applied, if any. It also shows you the total value of the invoice.

✔ **Global:** This section enables you to apply global terms to the whole of the invoice or credit note. If you chose to do this, only one line is added to the audit trail, although carriage is always shown as a separate line.

You can apply one nominal code to the whole invoice. If you do, you can also enter details to accompany the posting to the nominal ledger. Up to 60 characters are available for additional details, which appear on your reports.

The same global effect can be applied to your tax code and also your departments (if required).

✔ **Tax Analysis:** The tax analysis for each product item appears at the bottom of the Footer Details tab. The list shows a breakdown of all the VAT into the separate VAT codes (assuming the Global Tax option hasn't been used).

Credit notes are prepared in a very similar way to product and service invoices. The screens look exactly the same; however, after you type in the details of the credit note, the font becomes red.

Follow the same principles as you do to create an invoice, but make sure that you change the Type box on the Details tab to credit note. Refer back to previous sections of this chapter for assistance.

You need to remember to update your credit notes in the same way as you do invoices. If you don't, the credit notes aren't updated to the nominal ledger.

Editing the service invoice with the F3 key

When you press F3 from the Description line of an invoice, an edit box appears where you can amend some of the detail of your invoice. The nominal code, tax code and department all appear in the posting details in this edit box. The details shown are those chosen as defaults. You can amend both the tax and nominal codes for each item line on the invoice by using the dropdown list. Alternatively, if you want to use the same nominal code and tax code for all lines of the invoice, you can click the Footer Details tab of the invoice and enter the appropriate codes in the Global section. The new codes then overwrite any code used on an individual line of the invoice.

Communicating is Key

Communication and credit control are key to the success of any business. With this is mind, Sage has a revamped Communications tab (previously known as Contacts). Upon opening the Communications tab, you can record details of telephone calls, emails, letters or meetings and record follow-up actions. This function is particularly useful for credit controllers as they can record follow-up phone calls to customers, and Sage makes diary entries to remind them of their future tasks.

A new button on the navigation bar called Diary lets you access and view any appointments or follow-up calls made via the Communications screen.

Managing Your Invoice List

After you safely save an invoice, it appears on your Invoice list, and you can do all sorts of business-like things with it. The next sections tell you how.

Printing

As soon as you save your invoice, you can print it. If you still have the invoice open in front of you, simply click Print. The Invoice Printing window appears, displaying different print layouts. If you haven't got the invoice open in front of you, click Customers from the navigation bar and select Invoice List from the Links list. Highlight the invoice you want to print from the list and click the Print icon to open the Invoice Printing window.

Updating

After you are 100 per cent happy with your invoices, you're ready to *update,* a process that posts the invoice to both the nominal ledger and the customer ledger.

You can update invoices individually or in batches from your Invoice List. There are two columns which show you whether the invoice has been printed or updated. To update, you simply highlight the relevant invoice and click *update*. This will put a Yes in the Posted column.

You've now updated your invoice, and an Update Ledger report appears on your screen. You can print this if you want to, but it isn't really necessary.

Deleting

Deleting invoices and credit notes is easy, but be aware that if you've already posted the invoice to the nominal ledger, deleting the invoice or credit note doesn't reverse the posting in the ledger.

To delete an invoice or credit note, from Customers, click Invoice List. Select the required invoice or credit note from the Invoice list and then click Delete. An affirmation message appears. Click Yes to continue or No to exit.

That's it; your invoice is deleted from the Invoice list.

Saving Time while You Ask for Money

When creating invoices, it's useful to know about some of the time-saving features that you can use.

Duplicating existing invoices

If you need to send the same invoice details to a number of different clients, this function is very useful. From the Invoice list, highlight an existing invoice and click Duplicate at the bottom of the screen. The system produces an exact replica of the original, but you can edit the details, for example, change the dates and customer. Check all the details of the invoice before saving and amend where necessary.

Repeating recurring transactions

This feature is useful if you're invoicing the same product or service on a recurring basis. After you set up your recurring transaction, you can then continue to process the invoice in the same way.

To set up a recurring sales invoice, all you need to do is, create an invoice (see previous section) and click the *memorise* button. You must provide a reference and description for your recurring item. Decide the frequency – is it every day, week or month, and when does it start and finish? Once saved, and you start the routine of recurring invoices, the system will also tell you when that invoice was last processed.

Every time you open Sage, you're asked if you want to post your recurring entries. Choosing Yes posts the transaction, but choosing No allows you to use your program without posting the transactions.

You can turn this reminder off by clicking Company⇨ Company⇨Preferences⇨Parameter tab and then select the No Recurring Entries at Start-up check box.

To process the recurring transactions, you click the *Recurring* icon on the invoice list. The Memorised and Recurring Entries box appears. Then, simply select the item you want to process and click the *process* button. You then simply select the appropriately dated transaction that you wish to process. Make sure that all the transactions you want to process have a green tick in the box next to them. If you don't want to include a transaction, make sure that the box doesn't have a tick in it. Finally click the *process* button and voila it's done!

Using defaults

You may have invoices or credit notes that have similar items or characteristics, and as such you can enter defaults for them. For example, you may want to assign carriage costs to your customers.

To access the defaults, within Customers, scroll down the Links list and click Invoice/Order Defaults. To adjust carriage defaults, click Footer Details.

For help with other invoice defaults, select Help from the main toolbar and then click Contents and Index and select Invoices followed by Defaults.

Chapter 7

Dealing with Paperwork from Your Suppliers

. . . .

In This Chapter

▶ Getting and posting bills

▶ Entering credit notes

▶ Recording supplier payments

▶ Sending remittance advice notes

. . . .

*Y*ou receive lots of invoices from your suppliers, so you need to put systems in place so that you can easily locate the invoices if required. Sometimes Sage contains enough detail to answer a query about an invoice, but on some occasions you need to pull the actual invoice out of the file.

As you process each invoice, Sage allocates it a sequential number. Use this sequential number as a reference, so you can always track down an invoice quickly and easily.

Receiving and Posting Invoices

You need a system for capturing the purchase invoices that come into your business so that bills get paid and you can continue doing business. The two steps in making sure that this gets done are receiving the invoices properly and then posting them.

Setting up a receiving system

Send all invoices to one person or department (depending on the size of the business). You don't want lots of different people receiving the invoices as more people mean more chance of invoices getting misplaced or entered incorrectly. Enter invoices onto the accounting system as soon as possible after receiving them to record the liability in the business accounts. Depending on the business size, you may want to make a copy of the invoice to keep one in the Accounts department and send the other copy to the person who requested the goods, so that they can check the details for accuracy and get the invoice authorised for payment.

Posting invoices

The term *posting* doesn't mean posting the invoice into a letter box! In accounting terms, *posting* means processing an invoice to the nominal ledger. (Chapter 2 talks about the nominal ledger.)

You can post a number of invoices in one sitting. If you have large quantities of invoices to process, separate them into smaller batches and total the values of each batch so that you can check those same values against Sage to ensure that you haven't made any mistakes.

Users of Sage Accounts Professional have two different ways of posting invoices:

✔ If you receive an invoice as a result of raising a purchase order, you can update your order details and Sage automatically posts the invoice. See Chapter 11 for more information about purchase order processing.

✔ If you don't have an order for your invoice, you need to use the Batch Entry screen to process your invoice – a method I describe in the following steps.

Sort the invoices into date order before separating them into batches. This ensures that they get entered in chronological order, which helps when you are viewing them on screen.

Memorising and recalling batch invoices/credit notes

You can use the Memorise and Recall functions in Sage Accounts Plus and Professional versions to save you having to re-enter the same information again and again. For example, if you regularly buy the same product from the same supplier, you can use the Memorise function to save time when ordering the product.

Another great function is the ability to memorise a batch of invoices that you are in the middle of, so that

you can come back and amend them later. You can save the batch, go away and check some details and then come back, recall the batch, make the amendments and post.

To memorise a batch of invoices from within the Batch Entry screen, click Memorise, add a filename for the batch and click Save. To recall a batch of invoices, click Recall from within the Batch Entry screen, select the appropriate file and click Open.

To enter a batch, follow these steps:

1. **From Suppliers, click the Invoice icon.**

   This brings up the Batch Suppliers Invoice box.

2. **Select the correct supplier account for the invoice.**

   When you have several items on an invoice, enter each item from the invoice separately on the Batch screen as you may need to give each item a different nominal code. However, you can use the same supplier account, date and reference, so that Sage can group those items together.

   After you post the invoice, you can view it on the Supplier Activity screen, which is split into two parts. The top part has one line entry for each transaction (in other words all the individual lines of each invoice are grouped together), and the bottom part has the detail of each transaction. Clicking an invoice highlights it in blue, and the bottom part of the screen shows each line entry of that invoice.

3. **Put the invoice date in the Date field.**

   Be careful as Sage automatically defaults to today's date, so you need to overtype the invoice date here. If you don't, Sage won't age the invoice correctly, and you'll have a distorted view of the transaction on the Aged Creditors reports.

4. **Enter your sequential number in the Ref (Reference) field.**

   Your *invoice reference number* is the number order in which you file your invoices.

5. **Add details in the Ex Ref field, if desired.**

   You can add more references here or leave this field blank.

6. **Select the nominal code in the N/C field, using the dropdown arrow.**

7. **Click the department applicable for your invoice in the Dept field.**

   You can leave this field blank if you don't have any departments set up.

8. **Click the dropdown Project Ref arrow to select the appropriate project, if applicable.**

9. **Enter the Cost code if you are using project costing.**

   See Chapter 13 for further details on project costing.

10. **Enter information describing what the invoice is for in the Details field.**

    Put as much detail as you can here. I usually put the supplier's invoice number first followed by the description. You can then identify the invoice quickly using the supplier's number. If you need to contact them about an invoice, it helps to use their reference numbers, so it makes sense to record it here.

    Note: You can use the Ex Ref field for this purpose, but that field doesn't show up on every report.

11. **Enter the amount net of VAT in the Net field.**

12. **Choose the tax code applicable for this invoice in the T/C (Tax Code) field.**

Depending on the tax code, Sage updates the VAT field.

Make sure that the VAT Sage calculates is the same as the amount on the invoice. Sometimes Sage rounds up the VAT, and you need to overwrite the VAT amount in Sage to match the VAT on the invoice.

13. **Repeat steps 2 through 12 for each invoice in your batch.**

14. **Check that the total of your batch of invoices matches the total in the right corner of the Batch Entry screen (see Figure 7-1), and if they do, click Save.**

Doing the check ensures that the data you entered is accurate. When you click Save, Sage posts the invoices to the nominal ledger, posting a debit to the Cost account and a credit the Creditors control account.

Figure 7-1: A batch of purchase invoices entered onto Sage prior to posting.

Check out Chapter 18 to see how the function keys can help speed up the batch-entry process.

Getting Credit

Credit notes can be raised for a variety of reasons. The goods delivered may have been faulty or the wrong colour, for example. The supplier assumes that you have already posted the original invoice supplied with these goods and sends a credit note to reduce the amount you owe them. The credit note may completely reverse the value of the original invoice or partially credit the invoice.

Processing a credit note is done in much the same way as processing an invoice, so follow the steps in the previous section, 'Posting invoices', paying special attention to the following points:

✔ **From Suppliers, click the Credit icon instead of the Invoice icon and select the account to enter the credit note against.** The screen looks very similar to that of the Invoice screen, but the font colour is red rather than black, to help alert you to the fact that you are processing a credit note. You wouldn't be the first person to merrily continue entering credit notes, when they should be invoices!

✔ **Remember to change the date, unless today's date is acceptable.**

✔ **Enter a credit number instead of a ref number.** Use a unique sequential numbering system for your credit notes. Some people prefer to have a separate numbering system for credit notes, others just use the next available invoice number. It really doesn't matter, as long as you're consistent.

✔ **Make sure the nominal code (N/C) is the same as the invoice you're reversing.** This ensures that the correct cost code is reduced in value.

✔ **Put some notation in the Details field.** Something like 'Credit note against Invoice No 123' with a description as to why it is necessary, if possible.

✔ **If the credit note is reversing just part of an invoice, apportion the Net and VAT amounts.**

When you click Save, Sage posts the credit note, crediting the Purchase account and debiting the Creditors control account.

You can check to see if everything is posted by viewing the Activity screen for the nominal code you used.

Allocating a Credit Note

You allocate credit notes the same way you make payments, though you need to allocate a credit note specifically against an invoice.

You can tell if something hasn't been allocated if a transaction in the Supplier Activity screen has an asterisk against it.

To allocate a credit note, follow these steps:

1. **From Bank, click Suppliers.**

2. **Select the account you require.**

   All outstanding transactions are shown.

3. **Enter the date, usually the date of the credit note.**

4. **In the Payment column, click Pay in Full Against the Credit Note.**

   This puts a negative value in the Analysis total at the bottom right side of the screen.

5. **Move up to the invoice that you wish to allocate the credit note to. Type in the value of the credit note.**

   The Analysis total becomes zero.

6. **Click Save.**

   This posts the allocation, as shown in Figure 7-2.

Figure 7-2: Allocating a credit note to a supplier invoice.

Paying Your Suppliers

When you come to process the payments for your supplier, you need to use the Bank module.

1. **From Bank, select Suppliers.**

   A screen that looks a bit like a cheque book opens up.

2. **Check that the Bank A/C Ref field shows the correct account.**

   This field automatically defaults to account 1200, which is usually the Bank Current account. If this isn't the account you wish to use, select the appropriate account.

3. **Enter the supplier name or use the dropdown arrow to select the payee.**

   As soon as you select an account, Sage brings up a list of outstanding transactions for that account.

4. **Enter the payment date in the Date field.**

   Usually you use the date on your cheque stub or the date of the direct debit or other form of payment.

5. **Record the cheque number or method of payment in the Cheque No field.**

   Type **DD** for direct debit, **BP** for bank payment or any other short description that helps you identify the transaction when you reconcile your bank account.

6. **Click the Payment column.**

   You have several options here:

   - **To pay in full,** click the Pay in Full button at the bottom of the screen. This puts an amount in the £ box at the top of the screen, as Figure 7-3 shows.

     Note: If you're taking a discount for early payment, enter the discount amount in the Discount column, and Sage calculates the amount you owe and shows this value in the £ box and in the Payment column.

   - **To pay part of an invoice,** enter the amount you wish to pay against that invoice. That amount shows up in the £ box at the top of the screen.

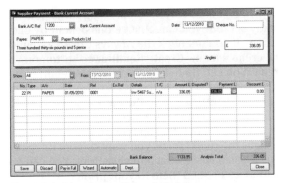

Figure 7-3: A happy supplier, paid in full.

- **To make a payment on account,** enter the amount you wish to pay in the £ box.

  You may find that you need to make a payment against a supplier account, but can't specify an invoice to allocate the payment to. You can make a payment onto the supplier account without matching it to a specific invoice.

7. **Click Save.**

  If you make full or partial payments to an invoice, the payment posts to that invoice in the supplier account. If you make a payment on account, Sage gives you a confirmation message, asking There is an unallocated cheque balance of £x. Do you want to post this as a payment on account? Click Yes to accept or No to cancel.

Printing a Remittance Advice Note

You may want to print a remittance advice note to accompany your cheque. A *remittance advice note* tells your supplier which invoices you're paying. Alternatively, you can just make a note of the invoice numbers on a compliments slip.

If you selected Always Create a Remittance in your Bank defaults, the system automatically stores a remittance for you. When I loaded my version of Sage, this default was already set, but you can change this default by clicking Bank Defaults. If you uncheck the Always Create a Remittance box, Sage creates a new Create Remittance button on you Payment screen. You can then selectively create remittances.

To print a remittance from the Bank module, click Remittance, and Sage lists all the remittances generated, whether manually or automatic (depending on how you've set your defaults). Highlight the remittances you want to print or select the date range if you have several and click Print. You can preview the remittances or send them to your printer.

Chapter 8

Recording Your Bank Entries

- -

In This Chapter

▶ Looking at the different types of bank accounts

▶ Processing bank receipts and payments

▶ Dealing with bank transfers

▶ Setting up recurring transactions

▶ Keeping track of petty cash

▶ Balancing credit card transactions

- -

*I*f you're the sort of person who likes checking their bank accounts and keeping track of what's been spent on the company credit card, then this chapter is for you! Here I tell you how to process bank payments and receipts that aren't related to sales invoices or purchase invoices. I look at how to process credit card transactions and deal with petty cash (one of the bookkeeping jobs that can be a real pain in the backside if not dealt with properly!)

I also show you how you can transfer money between bank accounts – perhaps to take advantage of earning some extra interest (every little helps!). And, as many businesses often have a lot of banking transactions, I show you ways to speed up the processing by using recurring entries.

Understanding the Different Types of Bank Accounts

Clicking Bank shows you the default bank accounts that Sage provides, which include:

- ✔ **Bank accounts:** Current, Deposit and Building Society accounts, for example.
- ✔ **Cash accounts:** For example, Petty Cash account.
- ✔ **Credit card accounts:** These include a Credit Card Receipts account for those of you who receive customer payments via credit card.

You can, of course, add new bank accounts, rename existing accounts or delete accounts you don't think you need – refer to Chapter 3 to find out how.

In the following sections, I show the account number or range of account numbers Sage assigns to each account. These account numbers are the same as the nominal code for that bank account.

Keeping up with the Current and Deposit accounts (1200/1210)

The Bank Current account is the default bank account in Sage, the one that automatically pops up when you enter a bank transaction. Of course, you can choose another bank account if the Bank Current account isn't the right one for your transaction.

Most people use the Bank Current account for the majority of their transactions, although you may have additional bank accounts for different areas of your business. Maybe you have a deposit account for surplus funds.

 Change the name of the Bank Current account to that of your own business current account, and if you have more than one, include the account number within the bank account name – for example, Barclays Current Account 24672376. You can add or amend bank accounts – for more information, refer to Chapter 3.

Counting the Petty Cash account (1230)

Use the Petty Cash account for cash stored somewhere other than a bank or building society – a strong box or safe in the office perhaps (*not* under your mattress!).

You can operate this account in the same way as a normal bank account, although most people don't choose to reconcile it as you don't have bank statements to reconcile to.

You can transfer funds into this account from any of the other Sage bank accounts and make payments accordingly. I give further details in the upcoming 'Dealing with Petty Cash' section.

Handling your Cash Register (1235)

You now have a separate bank account to handle your cash register transactions. Your business may wish to use this cash register function to record receipts of cash and card payments. This type of transaction allows for the sale, supply and payment to happen at the same time. A Cash Register sale can include details of the sale and the method of payment used (cash, cheque or card), the price and VAT (if applicable).

The default bank account is automatically set at 1235. You will need to check your cash register settings in your Bank Default menu. Click on Bank then settings then bank defaults. Here you can select the sales nominal code for your cash register takings, which automatically defaults to 4000 (you can change this). When using a cash register you may find that you have discrepancies between the cash register and actual takings. If so, use the discrepancy account to balance the books – the default code is 8206 (which can also be changed if you wish). There's also a tick box to confirm whether your cash takings are VAT inclusive or not.

For further help in using the cash register function within Sage you can click on 'What's New' on the Welcome screen and follow the guidance for Recording Till Takings.

Managing the company credit card (1240) and credit card receipts (1250)

You can set up a bank account for each individual credit card and manage these accounts as normal bank accounts – reconciling them, for example, with your credit card statements. See 'Paying the Credit Card Bill' later in this chapter for further details about the mechanics of processing credit card transactions.

If you accept payment by credit card, keep a separate bank account for these transactions. You deposit batches of credit card vouchers into your account in the same way that you deposit a cheque. Use the Customer option if you receive money against a customer invoice. The credit card company then deposits the real cash into your nominated bank account, and you can make a transfer between that and the Credit Card Receipts account. You then receive a statement detailing all the transactions, including a service charge, which can be reconciled.

Tracking Bank Deposits and Payments

Your business earns money (which is a good thing, and much better than the reverse!). You need to keep track of how much money you put in the bank and Sage helps you do that in the Bank module. You may also have to make payments to the bank – wages, interest charges, loan payments and dividend payments, for example. Sage makes it as easy to process a bank payment as it does a receipt.

For both types of transactions, start from the Task pane within the Bank module:

- ✔ For receipts, click New Receipt. Alternatively, click the Receipt icon.
- ✔ For payments, click New Payment or use the Payment icon.

In both cases, a new window appears and although the screens are different, they ask you for the same basic information whether you're recording a receipt or payment. Use the Tab key to move across the screen and enter the details Sage asks for:

- **Bank:** Make sure you select the correct bank account, using the dropdown arrows. Sage automatically defaults to account 1200, which is normally the Bank Current account.

- **Date:** As usual, Sage defaults to today's date, so ensure that you change this to match the date of the transaction.

- **Reference (Ref):** If you have a cheque number, pay-slip reference or BACS (Bankers' Automated Clearing Services) reference, enter it here as it proves very useful when you come to reconcile your bank account.

  When making a payment, be aware that the reference you enter appears on the audit trail in the Reference (Ref) column for that transaction, so use notation you can understand – *DD* for direct debit or *SO* for standing order, for example. If you paid by cheque, enter the cheque number here.

- **Nominal Code (N/C):** Using the dropdown arrow, select the appropriate nominal code. You can create a new nominal code here if you need to.

- **Dept:** Enter the department, using the dropdown arrow. Ignore this field if you don't use departments.

- **Project Ref:** Enter your project reference here. When the transaction is saved, your program updates the project activity and analysis information.

  And if you're making a payment, enter the relevant cost code.

- **Details:** Record any details that may help you with reconciling your account or identifying the transaction.

- **Net:** Enter the net amount of the transaction before VAT.

  If you aren't VAT registered, put the gross amount here and tax code T0, or T9 if you don't want it to appear on a VAT Return report.

  If you only have the gross amount of your receipts or a payment, you can enter this number and then click Calc Net (at the bottom of the Bank Payments/Receipts box) and, provided that the tax code is set correctly, the Sage calculates the net and VAT amounts for you.

 ✔ **Tax Code (T/C):** Use the dropdown arrow to select the
    appropriate tax code.

 ✔ **Tax:** Sage calculates the amount of VAT for the transac-
    tion based on the net amount and the tax code selected.

Whatever your business type, all businesses receive monies
that have nothing to do with their customers, such as bank
interest or grants. Post these payments using the Bank
Receipts option.

You can continue to enter receipts or payments in a batch.
Figure 8-1 shows a Payment Batch Entry screen. As you enter
new transactions, the total in the right corner of the screen
increases. Check the batch total you calculated against the
total Sage reached in the Total box in the top right of the
screen.

The boxes at the top of the screen show which bank account
the receipt is going to, what the nominal code is and the tax
rate. A Total box that subtotals all the lines of information in
the batch also shows.

Figure 8-1: A Payment Batch Entry screen.

When you're happy that the details on the screen are correct,
click Save at the lower left of the screen to post payments to
the appropriate nominal accounts and bank accounts. If you
aren't happy with the information on your Batch Entry screen,
simply click Discard and the information clears. To exit the
Payment Batch Entry screen, click Close.

Transferring Funds between Accounts

Just as big banks move money around, you may occasionally want to move money from one account to another. For example, when you pay off your company credit card each month, you make a payment from your current account to your credit card account. Create a bank transfer between the two accounts to process this transaction easily.

To process a bank transfer, from the Bank module click the Transfer icon and complete the details of the transfer. Using the drop down arrows, select which bank account the transfer is coming from and going to. You can add a personalised reference if you wish, and add details such as departments. The most important information however, is the date and amount! When you save this information, Sage updates both accounts.

Repeating Recurring Entries

Designating recurring entries is extremely useful. Doing so speeds up the processing of data and saves time because you enter the information only once, at the set-up stage, and then process all future transactions with the click of a button. You don't have to re-enter the full details of those transactions again!

You can treat many different transactions as recurring items, although they're typically direct debits and standing orders. The next sections give you an explanation of the different types of transactions you can set up as recurring.

Going for consistency with your bank entries

You probably make regular payments into and out of your Bank Current and Credit Card accounts, as well as doing transfers between accounts on a monthly basis. To set up any of these types of transactions as recurring, from Bank click New Recurring Transaction from the Task pane (or click the Recurring icon and then click Add). This opens the Add/Edit Recurring Entry box (see figure 8-2). You then simply fill in the details of the transaction you wish to complete and save.

Figure 8-2 shows a recurring entry that has been set up to process a direct debit that occurs every month from the bank current account for an insurance payment. You can do the same for any regular receipts that you may get.

Figure 8-2: Creating a recurring bank payment.

Repeating customer and supplier payments

If a customer pays you regularly (and I hope they do!) or you pay your suppliers regularly (ditto!), set up these recurring payments according to the process I outline in the preceding section, particularly if it's for the same amount each time (although it doesn't have to be the same). However, you must realise that this will only post the payments and receipts on account. You must allocate the receipts or payments to the specific invoices as a separate exercise.

Making regular journal entries – if you dare

This option is useful if you have to make an adjustment to the accounts where only a journal is possible. For example, if you make regular payments on a loan, rather than just setting it up as a bank payment, you can set it up as a journal and record both the payment and the interest (the specific journal depends on how the loan has been set up).

I advise using this only if you're confident about using double-entry bookkeeping. If you aren't competent with your book-keeping, it's dangerous territory!

1. **From Bank, choose New Recurring Transaction from the Task pane.**

   The Add/Edit Recurring Entry box appears.

   Although you enter your debit and credit transactions separately, you need to ensure that your journal entries balance, otherwise you get an error message. So, for every debit entry, you need to make a credit entry of the same amount.

2. **Enter the transaction information in the boxes.**

   You need to enter:

   - **Transaction Type:** Select either Journal Debit or Journal Credit.

   - **Nominal Code:** Using the dropdown arrow, select the nominal account to use. The name of the nominal account appears in the box next to the code selected.

3. **Complete the transaction details, posting frequency and amounts fields, as shown in Steps 4 through 6 in the previous section, 'Going for consistency with your bank entries'.**

4. **Click OK if you're happy with the journal details or Cancel if you're not.**

Your newly created recurring entry now appears on the Recurring list.

Processing and posting recurring entries

After you've set up recurring entries, every time you start up Sage, you're asked if you want to process your recurring entries. In the main, answer no at this stage, as it's better to process them in a controlled manner.

You can turn off this reminder by selecting the No Recurring Entries At Start Up check box in the Parameters tab of Company Preferences (click Settings and then Company Preferences).

You normally process your recurring entries just prior to reconciling your bank account so that they're ready and waiting to be reconciled.

To process your recurring transactions, you need to:

1. **From Bank, click Recurring List in the Links list.**

2. **Click Process.**

   The Process Recurring Entries box displays the message: Show recurring entries up to:.

3. **Enter the date you want to process recurring entries up to.**

   Normally, use the month-end date. For example, if you're about to reconcile the bank account to 30 April 2010, put in that date.

   After you enter the date, Sage shows you the recurring entries due to be posted up to the chosen date.

4. **Click Post.**

Sage doesn't post recurring entries with a zero value. Cancel the Posting screen and go back and edit the recurring entry so that a value is entered or choose to suspend the item.

Dealing with Petty Cash

Petty cash, funds kept in the office for incidental expenses, can often be an absolute pain to administer. Normally a company has a petty cash tin, which usually contains a small amount of cash and is stuffed full of receipts. As members of staff are given money from the petty cash fund, they exchange the money with a receipt. If you count up the amount of cash and receipts, the total of both should equal the value of the petty cash float. Unfortunately, some people request £20 from petty cash to buy some stationery, return with the receipt, but forget to return the change! The following sections tell you how to keep the petty cash tin in order.

Funding petty cash

Normally, you write a cheque out for petty cash or take the cash out of the bank and put it into the petty cash tin. To account for this within Sage, you can easily show this transaction as a bank transfer.

To do this, follow the instructions in the 'Transferring Funds between Accounts' section earlier in this chapter. Make sure that the Bank Current account is selected as the *account from* and the Petty Cash account is selected as the *account to*. If you wrote a cheque out for petty cash, you can use the cheque number as a reference.

Making payments from the tin

Make one person solely responsible for the petty cash tin. They can then ensure that if someone returns and doesn't have the correct change and receipts, at the very least an IOU goes into the tin for the money owed. That individual must get the money returned to the tin as soon as possible.

When a payment is made from the petty cash tin, make sure that a receipt replaces the money or use a petty cash voucher to record where the money has been spent. This ensures that all payments are correctly recorded and should also ensure that the petty cash tin balances to the agreed float amount.

To record a payment made from petty cash in Sage, follow the instructions for bank payments in the previous 'Tracking Bank Deposits and Payments' section, but select the Petty Cash account instead of the Bank Current account.

Reconciling the petty cash tin

Periodically, you need to reconcile the petty cash tin. The best time to do this is when you decide to top up the petty cash tin.

To do this, follow these steps:

1. **Extract all the petty cash receipts, batch them up and total them.**

2. **Give this batch a unique reference number, such as PC01 – you can use PC02 for the next batch and so on.**

   You can use this reference in the Reference field for recording the petty cash bank payments.

3. **Count the remaining petty cash.**

   The sum of this with the total from Step 1 should equal the petty cash float.

   If the petty cash float doesn't balance, check to see if anyone is holding back any petty cash receipts or if anyone has been given cash to do something and hasn't returned all the change or the receipts.

4. **Write a cheque for cash for the value of the receipts and use this to top up the petty cash float.**

   For all you teccies out there, this method is known as the Imprest system – you only replenish what you've spent.

Paying the Credit Card Bill

Many businesses use credit cards as a convenient way to purchase goods and services. And, just like other financial accounts, you need to include credit card payments in the monthly processing of transactions – after all, they can amount to quite significant amounts of money.

Making payments

After you receive the credit card statement, you need to match up the invoices and receipts with the statement:

- ✓ **Invoices:** If you paid a supplier using your credit card, you received an invoice, which has probably already been entered and filed away. In order to process this payment, just treat it as a supplier payment (refer to Chapter 7), but make sure you insert a reference to the method of payment somewhere. For example, in the Cheque No field use the reference *CC* for credit card. Alternatively, use a unique reference number for each credit card statement, particularly if several employees have their own cards. In this case, give the statement sheet for each individual its own unique reference number, such as *CC001*. This makes it easier to find the supporting papers for a transaction.

- ✓ **Receipts:** You may not have a proper invoice, just a till receipt for something purchased using the company credit card. In this instance, attach the receipt to the credit card statement and record the transaction as a bank payment. Make sure you select the Credit Card account as the account from which the payment is to be made. Also, make sure that you're careful with the VAT element of the payment; the amount of VAT attributable to a transaction isn't always obvious.

Reconciling the credit card statement

After you enter all the transactions from the credit card statement onto Sage, you are then in a position to reconcile the Credit Card account in the same way as a normal bank statement. (Chapter 14 talks about reconciling your bank account if you need a reminder.)

The only thing to remember when entering the credit card statement balance is that it is a negative figure, because it's money that you owe the credit card company.

The statement is usually paid via a direct debit from your bank account on a monthly basis, and you can treated it as a bank transfer between the Bank Current account and the Credit Card account, as described in the 'Transferring Funds between Accounts' section earlier in this chapter. You can reconcile the statement in the same way as any other bank account. Provided you enter all the transactions and set the statement balance to a negative figure, you can't go too far wrong!

Chapter 9

Maintaining and Correcting Entries

· ·

· ·

1 think it's fair to say that everyone makes mistakes. Sage understands this and makes it very easy for you to correct any mistakes. You can completely delete an item, change elements of a transaction, such as the date or tax code, or find an item in order to check something.

In this chapter, I show you how to make changes confidently to your data and correct mistakes where necessary.

Checking and Maintaining Your Files

You need to explore the file maintenance options. From the main toolbar, click File and then Maintenance. The File Maintenance box appears, as shown in Figure 9-1.

You'll sometimes experience data corruption when using Sage (but not often, I hope!) In the event that you incur any loss of monthly totals in your Nominal, Bank or Supplier records, you can use File ➪ Maintenance ➪ Recalculate monthly totals option to allow Sage to recalculate the monthly totals from your Audit Trail.

Figure 9-1: File maintenance options let you check and correct your data.

If you have used your Clear Audit Trail function at any point, do not use the recalculate monthly totals option, as it will not include any data prior to the Clear Audit Trail date.

The File Maintenance screen may look a little daunting, but you probably need to use only the Check Data and Corrections options with any regularity. I look at each function in the following sections.

Checking data

This facility allows you to check your data to make sure that it's not corrupt. It's a good idea to do this if your machine switches off in the middle of using Sage. Power cuts aren't unusual, and if you don't have an alternative power supply, Sage closes without being shut down properly, which can sometimes lead to corruption of data.

To start this process, click File and then Maintenance from the main toolbar, and then Check Data. The system checks each file, and if there are no problems, Sage gives you a message confirming that there are no problems to report.

Interpreting messages

If Sage finds any problems with your data, it brings up a box with several tabs that you can click for more information:

✔ **Comments:** The least serious messages, Comments simply alert you to the fact that your data may have inconsistencies.

✔ **Warnings:** Similar to Comments, in the sense that they often don't require data correction, Warnings alert you to problems that may require further investigation.

✔ **Errors:** An Error message indicates a problem with the data. You have the facility to fix these errors, but you must make a backup before you do this.

Personally, I'd be very concerned if I had errors in my data and would be tempted to restore my data back to a point where I knew the data was fine. (The 'Restoring Data' section later in this chapter tells you how to restore from a backup.)

Fixing data

You can correct most data problems showing errors via the Fix option. However, the corrective action used to rectify problems can be quite complex. If you're uncertain about the consequences of running the Fix option, seek help from Sage Customer Support, using the telephone number given to you when you took out SageCover.

Making corrections

Probably the most used of the file maintenance options, the Corrections button is a godsend to anyone who makes the odd mistake (including yours truly!).

Be warned that all actions you take are recorded in the audit trail, so your accountant can see how many corrections you've made. From an audit point of view, transactions need to be traceable even if you've made mistakes. Unfortunately, any deletions or changes to data are highlighted in red on the audit trail, so if you make wholesale changes to your data they stick out like a sore thumb!

Sage makes corrections to the individual transactions themselves, so it's important that you identify the precise transaction that needs correcting. You can find details on how to find transactions in the 'Finding Ways to Find Transactions' section later in this chapter.

You can't correct journal entries using the File Maintenance method. You can only correct journal entries by using a reversing journal from within the Nominal Ledger module. See Chapter 15 for details on how to do this.

To make a correction to a transaction, you can delete the whole transaction or correct a part of the transaction. From the File Maintenance screen, click Corrections to bring up the Corrections screen. Essentially, this screen shows a list of all your transactions in transaction number order. You must find the transaction you want to correct. At this point you have two options:

- **Edit Item:** Choosing this option opens the Making Corrections screen, which looks different depending on the transaction type. On the first screen, any item in black type can be changed. Click the Edit button to change greyed out items. You then have the option of changing most other parts of the data.

- **Delete Item:** If you know you want to delete an item, highlight it and click the Delete Item icon. The Deleting Transactions window appears. You can click the View button to see more of the transaction. If you are happy to delete it, click Delete.

That's how easy it is!

Re-indexing data

Sage recommends using the Re-indexing option only under the guidance of Sage Customer Support. When Sage recommends something like this, it's usually pretty serious! I can safely say that I've never had to do this, so I can only emphasise what Sage says: contact Customer Support if this need arises.

Compressing data

Compressing data files is also pretty serious stuff and outside the scope of this book. Briefly, this function basically constructs a new set of data files whilst removing deleted records, thereby reducing the file sizes. The files are compressed to create more disk space. As the compression procedure is irreversible, you need to take data backups beforehand, just in case any problems occur.

Rebuilding data

You need to tread carefully when using this part of the system because you can end up wiping all the data off your machine! (Mind you, if you take backups, which I explain in the 'Backing Up Data' section later in this chapter, you can restore it all fairly easily.)

You can chose to create new data files for all or part of the Sage Accounts system.

Click the Rebuild button, and the Rebuild Data Files window opens, with all the boxes ticked. A tick indicates that you don't want to create new data files for that part of the system. Removing the ticks tells Sage which parts of your software you want to create new data files for.

If you type **rebuild data files** into the Help menu, Sage guides you through the process of rebuilding your data files. However, have Sage Customer Support on standby, just in case anything goes wrong, so that they can talk you through the issues.

Use the Rebuild tool with extreme caution and always take a backup prior to attempting to do this.

Finding Ways to Find Transactions

Sometimes you need to find a transaction in order to correct or delete it. To find a transaction, you can use the Financials module, the Bank Reconciliation screen or the Corrections screen (in File Maintenance).

I demonstrate from the Financials module. Follow these steps:

1. **Using the navigation bar, click Company and then choose Financials from the Links list.**

2. **Click the Find button at the bottom of the Financials screen.**

   This brings up the Find box, shown in Figure 9-2, which, plainly enough, is what you use to find the transaction.

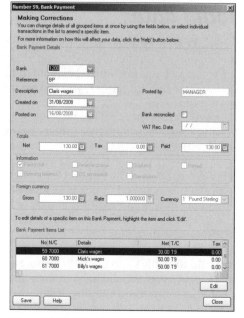

Figure 9-2: The Find box.

3. Enter details into the boxes.

Tell Sage what to find and where to look:

- **Find What:** The information entered here is dependent on what is shown in the Search In field (see the next point). For example, in Figure 9-2 the Search In field reads `Transaction Number`. So the entry in this Find What field should be a transaction number.

- **Search In:** A dropdown box gives you different variables that you can search with. The default variable is Transaction Number, but you can choose other alternatives. Your other choices are: Account Reference, Reference, Details, Date, Net Amount, Bank Account Reference, Nominal Account Reference, Ex Reference, Tax Amount, Amount Paid and Date Reconciled.

- **Match:** You don't have to search using the exact data; you have the option to select how close a match you can make.

Any: Finds all transactions that contain the details you entered anywhere in the field you are searching on. For example, if you're searching for an account reference and you enter RED, Sage finds references such as RED, REDMOND and CALLRED.

Whole: Finds the transaction that contains the exact details you enter in the Find What field. In this instance, when searching for account references, it brings up the RED account transactions.

Start: Finds all transactions that begin with the details you enter. So in the example, Sage would find transactions beginning with RED, such as RED or REDMOND, but it doesn't find CALLRED.

- **Case sensitive:** Check this box if you want Sage to find transactions that contain exactly the same upper and lower case letters as those entered in the Find What field.

4. **Click Find First.**

   If a transaction is found, Sage highlights it in blue. If this isn't the transaction that you're looking for, click Find Next.

   Note: You may need to cancel the Find box in order to see the transaction properly.

   If no transactions are found, a message to that effect appears. Click OK to return to the Find window so that you can enter new search details.

Searching for Records

You can search for records on Sage using the Search button in the Customers, Suppliers, Company, Products, Projects and Financials modules. The Search button is simply another method of tracing transactions.

I tend to search from the Financials module, as Sage performs a search on all the transactions from this module. If you search from the other modules, Sage limits the search solely to the information in that one module – which may be precisely what you want to do, in which case, have at it.

To perform a search from Financials, follow these steps:

1. **From Financials, click Search.**

   The Search box opens.

2. **Choose the variables to perform the search.**

   Your choices are:

   - **Join:** From the Join dropdown list, choose the Where option, which is the only option available. (And as Sage doesn't explain the connection between Join and Where, I can't either. It's just one of Sage's mysteries.)

   - **Field:** Click the Field column and select the variable you want to search by. In Figure 9-3, Total Amount Paid is selected.

   - **Condition:** Click the Condition column and choose a condition, such as *is equal to* or *is greater than*.

   - **Value:** Enter the value you want to search for.

     You can enter *wildcards,* which are special characters you can use to represent a line of text or an individual character. Click F1, the Help function key, whilst in the Search box, and Sage explains how to use wildcards.

Figure 9-3: Searching for – and finding! – £250.

Figure 9-3 shows a search for a transaction for the amount of £250. The screen behind shows that Sage found one transaction matching the search details.

3. **Click Apply.**

   Sage identifies all transactions that meet the conditions you selected. If Sage can't find a transaction, nothing comes up.

You can save a search so that you can find records with the same criteria later. Just follow the first two steps in the preceding list and then click Save instead of Apply. Enter a suitable filename and then click Save again. To access this saved file, open up the Search box, click Open and select the chosen file.

Backing Up Data

Performing regular backup routines is extremely important. If your data becomes corrupt or you need to reinstall Sage for whatever reason, you then have a backup that you can restore onto your machine, allowing you to continue working with the least amount of disruption.

To back up your data, follow these steps:

1. **From the toolbar, click File and then Backup.**

   A message asks if you want to check your data. Sage recommends that you check your data, which normally takes a matter of seconds, depending on how may records you have. Click Yes to check or No to continue with the backup.

2. **Make adjustments on the Backup window that comes up.**

   The Backup window contains three tabs:

   - The Backup Company tab, shown in Figure 9-4, displays the filename Sageback, today's date and the .001 file extension.

     Amend the filename with one that has meaning for your business. For example, the filename 'Jingles end of day Sageback 28-02-2009.001' indicates a backup of the Jingles card company's data as at close of business on 28 February 2009.

     Choose a location that you can find easily if you need to restore the data. Use the Browse button to change the location if you're not happy with the location Sage chooses.

• The second tab, Advanced Options, allows you to choose how much you back up. For example, you can include only data, or data plus reports, templates and so on. At the very least, back up your data files.

• The Previous Backups tabs holds – you guessed it! – previous backups.

Figure 9-4: The Sage Backup screen.

3. Click OK.

The backup starts, and when it's finished you get a confirmation message saying that the backup was successful.

Make sure that each backup has a different name. Sage makes this easy by adding the date to the file name, but if you perform more than one backup in a day, you have to change the name slightly, or otherwise a backup with the same name overwrites the first set of data.

Take backups at least at the end of every day, but if you're doing a large amount of processing, you may want to back up more often so that if you have to restore data you don't have to re-process too much information. Many people use a different disk, CD or pen drive for each day of the week, naming the backup disk Monday, Tuesday, Wednesday, Thursday, Friday. You can then restore information back to any day in your current week.

Restoring Data

Restoring data means that you erase the current data on the machine and replacing it with data from your backup disks.

Hopefully you won't need to run this routine, but if you do, follow these steps:

1. **From the main toolbar, click File and then Restore.**

   Sage tells you that it can't run this without closing windows. Click Yes, and the Restore window appears.

2. **Click Browse and select the file that you want to restore.**

3. **Click OK.**

   A message appears saying that you're about to restore and the process overwrites any data currently on the machine. Click Yes to continue or No to exit.

After successfully restoring your data, use the Check Data facility in the File Maintenance screen to check for errors. Refer to the 'Checking Data' section earlier in this chapter for advice on how to do this.

Part III
Functions for Plus and Professional Users

'Take me to your Financial Controller!'

In this part . . .

I take day-to-day transactions to the next level. Most of the chapters in this part are only for people who have Sage 50 Accounts Plus or Professional versions. I look at sales and purchase order processing, stock control and project costing.

This is pretty meaty stuff! You may dip into this part only occasionally, but all the information is here if you need it.

Chapter 10

Processing Sales Orders

● ●

In This Chapter

▶ Creating a quotation

▶ Writing up a sales order

▶ Apportioning stock

▶ Fulfilling orders

▶ Generating invoices

▶ Deleting and erasing orders

● ●

*S*ales order processing is available only if you have Sage
Accounts Professional. If you don't have this version, you
can skip this chapter. However, the first section on quotations
also applies to Sage Accounts Plus, so Plus users may want to
read this section.

Sales orders occur when a customer requests some of your
goods or services. In this chapter, I walk you through the
steps you follow to process a sales order, from the moment a
quote is confirmed through to allocating and despatching the
stock and then finally issuing an invoice to the customer.

Giving a Quote

I don't mean that your words are recorded for the enlighten-
ment of the masses! In the business sense, a *quotation* is what
you prepare when a potential customer asks for a price for a
product or service that you offer. You can create a quotation
within Sage that you can ultimately convert into an order if
the customer accepts your price.

Amending your invoice and order defaults

As an Accounts Plus user, even though you don't have Sales Order Processing as an option, you can still double-check the Invoice/Order defaults to ensure that your quotations raised are going to convert to a Sales invoice. Follow the instructions outlined here, but make sure that the Convert Quotes To field is set to Invoice.

Accounts Professional users also need to amend the Invoice/Order defaults. Whilst this may sound a bit scary, you're simply telling the system exactly how you want it to operate. For example, you can tell Sage exactly what number you want invoices and orders to start from – especially useful if you're continuing on from a previous system. Click the Options tab of the Invoice/Order defaults to make these changes in Sage.

To amend your Invoice/Order defaults **from** Customers, click Invoice/Order Defaults from the Links list. On the General tab, ensure that the Convert Quotes To field is set to Sales Orders. You can create an invoice later, which I explain in the 'Invoicing Your Customers' section later in this chapter.

Creating a quotation

After you check your defaults, you can create a quotation by clicking *New Quotation* from the Task pane of the Customer module. Using the dropdown arrows, select the account that you want to create a quotation for, and enter the details of the quote.

Access the Quotations list through Customers by clicking the Quotations list from the Links list. If you want to edit the details of any quote, from the Quotations list, highlight the quote you want to edit, click New/Edit, make the necessary amendments and click Save.

You can change the status of a quote by highlighting and right-clicking a quote from the Quotations list. Use the Set As options to change the status of a quote to open, won or lost.

Allocating and amending stock for a quote

You can allocate stock to an open quotation if you want. To allocate stock, simply select the quotation and click Allocate and then click Yes to the confirmation message that follows. If you want to amend the allocation of stock, select the quotation and click Amend. You can now adjust the amount of stock allocated.

Converting a quotation to an invoice or order

Depending on your Invoice/Order default settings, you convert your quotation to an invoice or to an order. I use the example of an order in the action steps throughout the rest of this chapter.

Accounts Plus users and those Professional users who don't want to convert a quotation to an order can convert it to an invoice instead. Follow the same steps as described in the next paragraph, but provided your Invoice/Order defaults are set to *Convert quotes to an invoice,* an invoice is created when you click Convert. You can look at the new invoice on your Invoice list (click Invoice List from the Links list within the Customer module).

From the Quotations list, select the quote that you want to convert and click Convert. Sage then asks you if you're sure that you want to convert the selected quote. Click Yes.

The status of the quote changes to *won,* and the quotation type becomes an *order.* A sales order is also created in the Sales Order list.

Creating a Sales Order

You can create a sales order in one of two ways: you convert a quotation as described in the preceding section, or you create a new order by clicking Customers from the navigation bar and selecting New Sales Order from the Task pane.

If you use the quotation method, you can access the new sales order after converting your quote by clicking Customers on the navigation bar and then the Sales Order list on the Links list. Highlight the order and then click the New/Edit icon.

Alternatively, if you clicked New Sales Order, the Product Sales Order window opens, which consists of six tabs:

✔ **Details:** This screen allows you to enter the main sales order details, including customer, dates, items ordered and prices.

✔ **Order Details:** You can amend the delivery details and add any notes about the order here.

✔ **Footer Details:** Use the Footer Details to enter information about carriage charges and use of couriers. It also includes a section on settlement terms and discounts.

✔ **Payment Details:** You can record a payment on the Payment Details tab. You can enter details of deposits already received or payments on account.

✔ **Despatched:** This tab shows the order status and details of any goods despatched notes. It only updates after you record a delivery of goods.

The main body of the despatched tab shows the goods despatched note number (GDN), the Customer's GDN and the date the goods were despatched. It also shows Y if the GDN has been printed and N if it hasn't. The despatched tab also contains the following information:

- **Order Status:** The status of the order appears here automatically. It may be *full, part, cancelled* or blank. If the status is blank, it's complete or has no stock allocated to it.

- **Despatch Status:** This box shows the despatch status of the order and can be *part* or *complete*. If no items have been despatched for this order, the box remains blank.

- **Invoice Status:** If you've raised an invoice for this order, the box contains *Y* for Yes. If you haven't yet raised an invoice, the box contains – you guessed it – *N* for No.

- **Complete:** If the order is complete, *Y* appears in this box. If the order is not yet complete, *N* appears here. (I'll let you figure out what *Y* and *N* stand for.)

- **Due Date:** You can enter an estimated despatch date here. However, if the sales order is complete, you can't amend this field.

- **Intrastat**: This box only appears if Intrastat reporting is enabled in the Invoice/Order defaults.

✔ **Invoices:** The last tab on the sales order shows which invoices are raised against an order. If you want to see the full details of the invoices, double-click the invoice from the list.

Entering the sales order details

As mentioned earlier, you can create a sales order from a quotation, but not everybody wants to issue quotations. If you want to create a sales order without first creating a quotation, follow these steps:

1. **From Customers, click New Sales Order from the Task pane.**

   The Details tab for a product sales order opens up.

2. **Enter the header details.**

   You're asked to select or provide information:

   - **Type:** Using the dropdown arrow, select Sales Order or Proforma Sales Order.

   - **Order Number**: Sage automatically assigns each order a sequential number after the order has been saved.

     The first order is given the number 1, the next the number 2 and so on. If you want to start from a different number, change the number on the Options tab on Invoice/Order defaults.

   - **Date:** Enter the date of the order. The system defaults to the current day's date, unless you change it.

- **Invoice Reference:** When you update your sales order to match an existing invoice, the last invoice number relating to the sales order appears.

- **Account:** Enter the customer account reference here.

- **Item Number:** The number of the item that's currently highlighted on the order. For example, if there are five item lines, and the cursor is currently on the second line, the box says Item 2 of 5.

3. **Complete the main body of the order by entering the product items that have been sold.**

   Enter the basic information about the products:

   - **Product Code:** Using the dropdown arrow, select the product code required. If you don't have a specific product code to use, you can use a special product code. (See Chapter 6 for more details on special product codes.)

   - **Description:** This field automatically updates when you select a product code. However, you can edit the description by pressing F3. Refer to Chapter 6 to find out more about using the F3 button.

   - **Quantity:** Enter the quantity of stock that the customer has ordered.

   - **Price:** The unit price from the product record appears here.

   - **Discount:** The customer discount amount for the item displays here.

   - **Discount percentage:** The percentage discount that the customer receives displays here.

   - **Net:** The net amount is calculated automatically. You can't change this value.

   - **VAT:** The VAT amount calculates automatically, and you can't change the value.

   - **Total:** The order is totalled at the bottom, showing the net value, an addition for carriage charges if they're applicable, the amount of VAT and finally, a gross amount.

- **Deposit:** This new feature has a smart link to the Payment tab of the order, allowing you to record any deposits received against the order. In addition, Sage 50 Accounts now gives you the option to Pay by Card, but you need to have registered for Sage Payment Solutions to use this feature. (Click Weblinks from main toolbar to find out more.)

- **Deduction:** This is also a new feature. Here, Net Value Discount offers a drilldown arrow in the Description box which, when clicked, reveals an Edit Item line. You can enter information referring to the discount and a discount value, and then press Tab – Sage then automatically calculates the percentage discount. If you enter a discount percentage, Sage calculates the value instead.

4. **Click the Order Details tab to add a delivery address or any notes to the order.**

Some information is pulled through from the customer record, such as telephone number and contact. A Sales Order Status section shows if stock's been allocated to the order and the delivery status of the goods. You can enter an estimated despatch date for the sales order if required.

5. **Click the Footer Details tab to add carriage details.**

The information requested includes assignment numbers and courier details:

- **Carriage terms:** You may want to assign carriage costs to the order as you may have postal or courier costs. You can set up specific nominal codes for charging the carriage costs. If you've set up departments, use the dropdown list to select the appropriate one. You can also add the consignment number and courier details and track your parcel by accessing the courier's website.

- **Settlement Terms:** Some information may already be present in these boxes, depending on what details you entered on your customer record.

- **Global:** This section allows you to apply global terms to the whole order. If you choose to use this option, only one line is added to the audit trail. However, carriage is always shown as a separate line.

You can choose to apply a global nominal code to the whole order. This global code is posted to the nominal ledger when you update the invoice that is eventually generated from the order.

You can also apply the same global option to your tax code and your departments (if required).

- **Tax Analysis:** The tax analysis for each product item is shown at the bottom of the Footer tab. The list shows a breakdown of all the VAT into the separate VAT codes (assuming the Global Tax option hasn't been used).

6. **Click Save when you're happy with the details you've entered.**

The Sales Order screen then reverts to a blank order. Please don't panic! Sage has saved your order, which now shows on the Sales Order list. You can find the Sales Order list from the Links list within Customers.

Dealing with cash sales

Some orders are completed at point of sale, particularly if you have over-the-counter sales. The customer pays for the goods and takes them away immediately. You can receive payment for cash sales online by using the Sage Payment Solutions wizard. (Type **Sage Payment Solutions wizard** into the Sage Help facility to find out more.)

Instead of manually completing each element of the Sales Order life cycle from stock allocation through to ledger update, you can automate the whole process by choosing the Cash Sales option when you're creating the sales order.

To activate the Cash Sales option, enter the sales order details, as shown in the preceding 'Entering the sales order details' section. Then click the Cash Sales button at the bottom of the order on the Details tab. A confirmation message asks if you wish to complete this order as a cash sale.

Click Yes to continue or No to return to the order. If you click yes, the system completes all stock allocations, creates an invoice and creates a bank transaction for the receipt of cash.

You must have sufficient stock levels to satisfy the whole order, although you can set Sage to allow negative stock values: the order then goes through regardless of stock levels.

You can limit the order paperwork produced for a cash sale to only those documents that you actually need, from Invoice/ Order defaults, click the Cash Sales tab, and select the documents you require.

To complete the order, Sage generates and allocates a sales receipt to it.

Editing your order

If you decide to change something after you create an order, you can easily amend the details of your order by highlighting the relevant order on your Sales Order List and click the New/ Edit icon at the top of the screen. This will open up the order which you can amend as you like. When you're happy with it, click Save.

Putting sales orders on hold

You may find that you need to put an order on hold while you check out the credit status of a new customer or see if you have enough stock. This is easily done from Customers, by clicking the Sales Order List from the Links list. You select the sales order you want to put on hold and click Amend. From the Amend Allocations screen, click Off Order. If you click *held* and then OK, you will be returned to the Sales Order Processing screen, where you can see that the status of the order is now *held*.

If you want to take the order off hold, highlight the order, click Amend and then click Order. Close the Amend Allocations screen. You've cancelled the on-hold status.

Duplicating a sales order

You can use the Duplicate facility to copy an existing order with the same details as those that you wish to enter for a new order. I use this time-saving device a lot when processing data.

To duplicate a sales order, you simply find a sales order that you wish to duplicate from the Sales Order List within Customers. Select the order and click duplicate.

A new sales order opens that's an exact copy of the previous order. Notice that it has a heading showing that it's a duplicate order. After you save the duplicated order, it acquires an order number of its own.

You can then amend any details that are necessary and click save to finalise your new order.

Printing the order

The print facility in Sage allows you to print as many copies of the order as you want. Just select the order that you wish to print from the Sales Order List and click Print. You can choose to preview, print, send to a file or email. I tend to preview the report first to ensure that the details are correct and that I'm happy with the layout.

Allocating Stock to an Order

After you create your sales order, you need to allocate your stock to it. If the order has already been despatched and you've completed the order, Sage automatically allocates the goods for you. Otherwise, the next sections describe how to apportion stock automatically and manually.

Going on automatic

Sage automatically allocates as much stock as possible to your orders, so the amount of *free stock* (stock available to fulfil orders) decreases and the amount of *allocated stock* (items earmarked for specific orders) increases.

To allocate stock automatically, follow these steps:

1. **From Customers, click Sales Order List, highlight the order to which you want to allocate stock and click Allocate.**

2. **Click Yes when Sage asks if you want to allocate all stock to the order.**

   If you don't have enough stock to allocate to the order, Sage lets you know.

   The Sales Order Processing window reappears, and the order shows the word *full* in the Allocated column. If there isn't enough stock to allocate to the order, the column reads *part*.

Assigning stock yourself

Allocating stock manually gives you greater control. For example, if you have two orders, each for ten boxes of cards, but you have only ten boxes in total, you can manually allocate five boxes of cards to each order and tell each customer that the balance of the order is to follow.

You can manually allocate stock by highlighting the relevant order on your Sales Order List and then click Amend. The Amend Allocations screen will open (as shown in Figure 10.1) and you can manually add the number of units to allocate to this order. To save your changes, click Close. The word *part* now shows in the Allocated column against that order.

Figure 10-1: The results of allocating stock for part of an order.

Sage then reduces the amount of free stock and increases the amount of allocated stock in the same way that it does if you automatically allocate stock. Figure 10-1 shows a partially allocated order.

Amending the allocation of stock

If you've allocated stock to an order but haven't despatched it, you can still amend the order and reallocate stock. Simply select the sales order from the Sales Order list and click Amend. You can then change the amount of stock you've allocated to that order.

Using the shortfall generator

Sage is an extremely intelligent program and can tell you if you don't have enough stock to fulfil all the orders raised.

To check your stocks, select the orders from the Sales Order list and click the Shortfall icon on the Sales Order Processing toolbar. The Shortfall Generator window shows a list of any products that have a stock level less than the quantity required for the order, as shown in Figure 10-2. If you click Create Order, you can generate a purchase order for the specific products you're running short of.

Product Code	Description	Supplier	BOM	ee/On-Order	Required	ShortFall	antity to Order
CARD-HB	Card - Happy Birthday			1140.00	5000.00	3860.00	3860.00

Figure 10-2: Predicting a shortfall is another handy Sage tool.

Despatching Orders

After you allocate the stock to the order, you're then ready to despatch the goods, using any one of the four methods Sage offers. The next sections explain each of these methods.

Completing an order

You complete your order when the goods have already been sent to the customer. In completing the order, Sage allocates stock to it and marks the order as being despatched. To complete an order, you need to highlight the order from the Sales Order list, click Edit to view the order and then click the Complete button (at the bottom of the Details tab). Depending on stock availability, your order is then marked *complete* or *part complete*.

Using goods despatched notes (GDNs)

This option automatically records the despatch of goods and provides maximum traceability because you can view all the GDNs on the Despatch tab for each order.

Before beginning to use GDNs, you need to set up your GDN options in the Options tab of Invoice/Order defaults. You have the following choices:

✔ **Generate for all despatches:** The default option. Sage gives you the choice of printing a GDN now or later.

✔ **Prompt at each despatch:** Sage prompts you each time you record a despatch as to whether you want to generate a GDN now or later. If you don't generate the GDN, Sage doesn't store the GDN in the Despatched tab of the Sales Order, so you can't view or print the note later.

✔ **Do Not Generate:** If you select this option, Sage updates your sales order and your stock level but doesn't produce a GDN.

Sage issues a GDN depending on the default options you select. You can raise a GDN by clicking the Despatch button, or you can click the GDN button. Details of both methods are outlined in the next sections.

Using the despatch facility

You can use the Despatch facility to record complete deliveries of orders to your customers. Follow these steps:

1. **From Customers, click Sales Order List from the Links list.**

2. **Select the orders from the Sales Order Processing screen and click Despatch.**

   Sage then generates a GDN (if this option is selected in your defaults), creates a product invoice and updates the stock level for each product on the order.

Recording a despatch manually

If you're not despatching the whole order, you can manually record the delivery of the stock you're sending. You need to use the Amend facility to record complete or part despatches; just follow these steps:

1. **From the Sales Order Processing window, click Amend.**

2. **Edit the quantity shown in the This Despatch column from within the Amend Allocations window.**

3. **Click Despatch to update the product records.**

   A prompt message comes up, shown in Figure 10-3, asking if you want to create invoice details, update stock and record the despatch for the previous order. Choose an answer:

   • **No:** Prints a delivery note only (according to the options chosen).

   • **Cancel:** Returns you to the Allocations screen, which you can close if you want to.

   • **Yes:** Allows you to continue with the despatch of the goods. Sage automatically generates an invoice, which shows on the Invoice tab of the order.

Figure 10-3: Recording a part despatch of an order.

Invoicing Your Customers

After you allocate and despatch all stock relating to your order, you need to print the invoices created from your order and update the ledgers to complete your sales order cycle.

When you despatch an order, Sage 50 Accounts automatically generates a product invoice for each order or partial order. The program also updates your stock levels at the same time.

You can check that Sage has raised an invoice by looking at the Invoice tab for your order to see the invoice number. You can view the invoice from the Invoice tab and then print it. Alternatively, you can print the invoice from the Invoice list. Highlight the invoice you want to print and click the Print icon. Double click the layout you prefer, and you can preview the invoice before printing.

When you're ready to update your invoices, from Customers, click the Invoice list. Select the invoices you want to post and then click Update. Sage posts the invoices to the sales and nominal ledgers.

Deleting and Cancelling Sales Orders

You can delete cancelled or completed orders as necessary and flat-out cancel orders as well.

To free up disk space on your computer, remove fulfilled or cancelled orders by compressing your data.

Before deleting orders, make sure that you carry out a backup in case you change your mind about the deletion and need to restore your data. I give details on how to do a backup in Chapter 9.

Orders can be easily deleted by clicking the Sales Order List from the Links list and selecting the order that you want to delete. Once you click Delete button, a confirmation message appears asking you to confirm that you want to delete. To continue with the deletion, click Yes.

When you delete an order, Sage deletes any goods despatch notes associated with that order. You need to be sure that you don't require GDN information before you delete the order.

You can cancel sales orders, as long as they don't have the status of *complete* in the Despatched column of the Sales Order Processing window.

After you cancel an order, it still remains on the Sales Order list, but its status changes to *cancelled.* Any stock that was allocated to that order reverts to free stock again.

To cancel a sales order, select the order from the Sales Order List and then click Amend. If you click Off Order when the Amend Allocations window appears. The Order Status window appears. To cancel your order, click Cancel Order. Click OK to confirm the cancellation, or if you decide you *don't* want to cancel the order, click Cancel.

When you cancel a sales order the Off Order button changes to Order. If you want to put a cancelled order back on order, click the Order button from the Amend Allocations window.

When you cancel an order, Sage cancels all the items in that order. If you want to cancel only a specific item on an order, choose the New/Edit icon from the Sales Order Processing window. Delete the unwanted item from the order, or press the F8 key to delete specific lines on the order.

Chapter 11

Processing Purchase Orders

● ●

In This Chapter

▶ Making up a purchase order

▶ Giving goods *on order* status

▶ Finishing up the purchase order process

▶ Accepting delivery of goods against your order

▶ Generating an invoice

▶ Cancelling and deleting purchase orders

● ●

*I*f you have Accounts Professional, Sage helps you process your purchase orders. If you don't have this version of Sage, you can skip this chapter.

You raise purchase orders for goods that you place on order with your suppliers. The purchase order processing system (POP) is directly linked to other parts of your system: it updates stock records and project records if you're using these parts of your system. In this chapter, I cover the stages that a purchase order goes through.

Creating, Changing and Copying a Purchase Order

When you order supplies, materials, widgets or similar, you need to create a paper trail – or at least an electronic trail – that you can send to your supplier to tell them what you need, how much, by what date and for what price. This paper trail is called a purchase order (or PO). Sage Accounts Professional has the perfect process for conveying this information.

Creating a purchase order

Creating a purchase order basically consists of completing information requested in four tabs; just follow these steps:

1. **From Suppliers, click New Purchase Order from the Task pane.**

2. **Fill in the information requested in the Details tab.**

   You're asked to provide basic information such as:

   - **Order Number:** Sage automatically issues each order a sequential number, although you don't see it until you save the order.

     The first order is given the number 1, the next the number 2 and so on. If you want to start from a different number, change the number on the Options tab on Invoice/Order defaults.

   - **Date:** Enter the date of the order. Keep in mind that the system defaults to the current day's date, unless you change it.

   - **Account:** Enter the supplier account reference.

   - **Project Reference:** This reference only shows when you've switched on Project Costing. Use the dropdown arrow to link the order with a specific project if so required.

   - **Cost Code:** This code only shows when you've switched on Project Costing. You can use the dropdown arrow to select a cost code.

   - **Reference:** You can enter an additional reference here if you like.

   - **Item Number:** This field shows the number of the item that is currently highlighted on the order. For example, if you have five item lines and the cursor is currently on the second line, the box says Item 2 of 5.

- **Rate:** The rate only appears if you've enabled the Foreign Currency option.

3. **Complete the main body of the order.**

   List the details of the product items that you want to purchase:

   - **Product Code:** Using the dropdown arrow, select the product code required. If you don't have a specific product code to use, you can use a special product code. Refer to Chapter 6 for more details on special product codes.

   - **Description:** The description updates automatically when you select a product code. However, you can edit the description by pressing the F3 key.

   - **Quantity:** Enter the quantity of stock that you want to order.

   - **Price:** The unit price from the product record appears here.

   - **Net:** This amount calculates automatically. You can't change this value.

   - **VAT:** This amount also calculates automatically, and again, you can't change the value.

   - **Total:** The order total appears at the bottom, showing net, VAT and any carriage charges applied.

4. **Click the Order Details tab to add a delivery address or any notes to the order.**

   Sage then pulls certain information from the supplier record, such as the supplier's telephone number and contact information.

5. **Click the Footer Details tab to add carriage details.**

   You can include assignment numbers and courier details here:

   - **Carriage Terms:** You may want to assign carriage costs to the order, or postal or courier costs. You can set up specific nominal codes for the carriage costs to be charged to. If you've set up departments, use the dropdown list to select the appropriate one. You can also add the consignment number and courier details and track your parcel via the courier's website.

Click Help from the main toolbar to set up a courier on your Footer Details tab. Using the Contents and Index option, type **couriers** to find out how to enter the appropriate details.

- **Settlement Terms:** Some information may already be present in these boxes, depending on what details you entered on your supplier record. You can enter the number of days during which an early settlement discount applies, if any. You can see what discount percentage is applied, if any, and the total value of the invoice.

- **Tax Analysis:** The tax analysis for each product item appears at the bottom of the Footer Details tab. The list shows a breakdown of all the VAT into the separate VAT codes.

6. **Click Save to preserve the order.**

   The Purchase Order screen then shows a blank order, but don't panic! Sage has saved your order and is ready for the next one.

As soon as you close the Purchase Order screen, you can view a copy of your order on the Purchase Order list.

Editing your order

If you decide to change something after you've created your order, you can amend the details of your order by clicking on your Purchase Order List and selecting the purchase order that you want to amend. If you then click the New/Edit icon at the top of the Purchase Order Processing (POP) screen, you'll bring up your order, which you can then amend as you wish. Click Save when you finish editing the purchase order.

Duplicating a purchase order

You can copy an existing order with the same details as those you want to enter for a new order. I use this duplicate feature a lot when processing orders – it speeds up the entry time. Duplicating an order is easy – just highlight the order you wish to duplicate from the Purchase Order List and click Duplicate. You edit any details and save the order. The Purchase Order list then appears, showing the new order.

Placing the Goods On Order

After you create a purchase order and are about to send it to your supplier, you need to put it on order with Sage as well.

Ordering conventionally

In the following steps, you change the status of the order to *on order* and update your on-order stock levels for the appropriate product codes. To do this:

1. **From Suppliers, click Purchase Order List.**

2. **Select the order that you want to place on order by clicking the Order icon in the POP screen.**

   A confirmation message appears, asking if you want to print the order. Click Yes if you want to print or No if you want to continue without printing.

3. **To place the goods on order, click Yes when asked if you want to place all selected items on order.**

   The POP window then reappears, showing the status of the order as *on order*.

Now, when the goods come in, you can receive them properly.

Ordering manually

An alternative method of placing your goods on order lets you view the order again prior to placing it on order – something the method described in the previous section doesn't allow. If you want to double-check the items on the order, follow these steps:

1. **Select the order from the Purchase Order list.**

2. **Click the Amend icon.**

You see all the product records contained within your order, one line per product.

3. **To put your purchase order on order, click Order. The full order quantity then appears in the This Delivery column.**

In Figure 11-1 note that the This Delivery column is currently zero on both the product lines. As soon as you place the goods on order, the value changes.

Figure 11-1: Manually placing goods on order allows you to check the order beforehand.

4. **Click Close to return to the POP window.**

The purchase order now shows on order.

Completing Your Purchase Order

Completing your order is necessary only if you've already received your goods. The process of completing your order means that Sage saves the order, completes the order and records the delivery of stock immediately.

If the order is linked to a project, Sage automatically allocates the goods to the project and then applies the costs. Sage applies actual costs at different stages, depending on the type of item ordered:

✔ **For a stock item:** Sage applies actual costs when the stock item is issued to the project.

> ✔ **For a non-stock or service item:** Sage applies actual costs when the invoice is recorded for the purchase order.

To complete your order, follow these steps:

1. **From Suppliers, click Purchase Order List from the Links list.**

2. **From the POP window, select the order that you want to complete and click the New/Edit icon.**

   This takes you into the Details screen of the order.

3. **Click Complete at the bottom of the screen and then click Yes when you get the confirmation message saying that you've selected to complete the order in full. Click Yes to continue.**

4. **Click Yes again when a further confirmation message appears, asking if you want to update stock and record delivery of the order.**

   Sage then generates a goods received note and asks if you want to print it now or later. Make your choice and decide whether to print the purchase order as well.

5. **Close the Purchase Order screen.**

   The screen returns to the Purchase Order list and the status of your order shows as *complete*.

If you look on the Deliveries tab of you order, you see that Sage has generated a goods received note (GRN). You can view or print the GRN from this screen.

Printing Your Purchase Order

You can print or spool a copy of one or more purchase orders so to send out to the suppliers or keep a hard copy for your records (although going paperless as much as possible is greener for the planet and cheaper for your company). *Print spooling* refers to the process of transferring data to a temporary holding place (a buffer, usually an area on a disk). The printer can pull the data off the buffer when required, leaving you free to carry out other computer tasks while the printing is done in the background.

Printing POs in batches makes sense, if only because you can put the correct stationery in the printer.

You can print a batch of purchase orders by selecting the purchase orders you want to print from your Purchase Order List, and clicking Print. When you've selected the layout you want, you can select the output you require. You can choose to print, preview, file or email.

Getting the Goods In

After you send a purchase order, you typically receive goods after a reasonable amount of time. (If you don't, you need to pursue the issue with the supplier!) When the goods arrive, you need to book them into Sage. If you placed the order for a project and completed the PO as described previously in this chapter, Sage automatically records the stock as delivered and allocates it to the proper project.

In the following sections, I cover three alternative ways of recording the delivery of goods.

Using goods received notes

A quick and easy way of recording the delivery of stock, goods received notes (GRNs) allow you to record deliveries against more than one order at the same time. Sage keeps a record of all GRNs raised against each order. You can view and print these by going to the Deliveries tab of each order.

Setting GRN defaults

To adjust the settings for GRNs, follow these steps:

1. **From Suppliers, click Invoice/Order defaults and then click the Options tab.**

2. **Amend the default setting for GRNs as needed by using the dropdown arrow.**

   Your options are:

- **Generate for all received:** The default option. Sage generates a GRN for each delivery, but gives you the option to print now or later.

- **Prompt at each received:** Each time you record a delivery, Sage asks whether to generate a GRN or not. If you choose not to generate the GRN, Sage doesn't store a copy of it, so you can't view or print it later.

- **Do not generate:** Sage updates the purchase order and stock levels, but doesn't produce a GRN. The GRN option doesn't appear on the Purchase Order Processing toolbar.

3. **Click OK.**

Generating the GRNs

If you selected the Do Not Generate GRNs option, ignore this section, as the GRN icon doesn't appear on your toolbar. If you want to process your GRNs, then read on:

1. **From Suppliers, click Purchase Order List and select the order for which you want to raise a GRN.**

2. **Click GRN.**

   Note: You can only use the GRN option if the status of the goods is *on order.*

   The Goods Received Note window opens.

3. **Enter the date and supplier information in the boxes provided.**

   As soon as Sage identifies the supplier, all the outstanding items from the selected purchase order appear, as shown in Figure 11-2.

   You may want to enter the supplier's GRN if you have it.

4. **Check the details. If the delivery is all there, click Receive All.**

   If not all of your order was delivered, enter the actual quantities received in the Received column.

   The Received column then changes from zero to the value of the items received.

Figure 11-2: Entering your goods received information.

5. To save the goods received information, click Save.

A message appears saying:

```
A goods received note has been gener-
ated for this order and stored under
the Deliveries tab of the order. You can
print this goods received note now, or
continue processing and print it from the
Deliveries tab of the order.
```

You can, if you want, tick the Do Not Show This Message Again box to deselect it.

If you don't want to save the goods received information, click Discard.

6. To return to the Purchase Order Processing window, click Close.

The status of the order changes to *complete* on the Purchase Order list, or to *part* if you received less than your full order.

Accepting delivery of everything

If everything on your purchase order comes in, you can use the Deliver function to record that, as long as you've already placed the PO on order (see the 'Placing the Goods On Order' section earlier in this chapter).

To accept delivery, follow these steps:

1. From Suppliers, click Purchase Order List.

2. **From the Purchase Order Processing window, select the order you want to process and click Deliver.**

   You receive a confirmation message asking if you want to update stock and record delivery of the items. Click Yes to continue.

   Depending on which GRN options you selected (see 'Setting GRN defaults' earlier in this chapter), you may get a message asking whether you want to print a GRN. Print as required.

   The Purchase Order window reappears, showing the status of the order as *complete.*

Taking in part of an order

You can use the Amend facility to manually record delivery of a complete or partial order. You have a chance to check the order line by line against what has been delivered instead of automatically updating and recording stock. Also, you can choose to process part or complete deliveries instead of being forced to record complete deliveries only.

Before you can amend your order, you must place it on order.

To use the Amend tool:

1. **From Suppliers, click Purchase Order List.**

2. **Highlight the order you want to change and then click Amend.**

   The Amend Deliveries window appears, showing the full order quantity in the This Delivery column.

3. **To record a partial delivery, amend the actual quantity received in the This Delivery column.**

   If you want to record a complete delivery, move to Step 4 without amending the This Delivery column.

4. **Click Deliver to update the product records with the new delivery information.**

   A confirmation message appears asking if you want to update the stock and record delivery of the items. Click Yes to continue or No to return to the Amend Deliveries screen.

Depending on the GRN options you chose, you may be asked to print your GRN.

5. **Click Close to return to the Purchase Order list.**

   If you received a partial order, the Purchase Order window now shows the new status of the order as *part.*

Creating an Invoice from an Order

As part of the life cycle of the Purchase Order process, ultimately you want to match the invoice received from the supplier to the order that you raised in Sage. Sage allows you to do this by converting the purchase order to an invoice by using the Update icon. This icon allows you to mirror the information from the invoice received from the supplier. You also save time, as you don't have to type in all the supplier invoice details, because most of it has already been entered at the order stage.

The purchase order has a Posted column. If it's blank, the order hasn't been posted to the purchase ledger. If the order's been updated, you see a *Y* in the column. When the order is updated, it posts to the purchase ledger and the nominal ledger.

You can update part-delivered orders. Each part creates its own invoice, so you may have more than one invoice relating to the same order.

To create a purchase invoice for a partially or fully delivered order, follow these steps:

1. **From Suppliers, click Purchase Order List.**

2. **Highlight the order(s) against which you want to raise an invoice and click Update.**

   If you've enabled transaction email and linked the selected orders to a supplier record that's marked `I send orders to this supplier electronically`, a prompt appears asking you whether you want to send the orders now.

The Purchase Order Update window opens.

3. **Edit any of the details shown in the Purchase Order Update window by highlighting the lines you want to change and clicking Edit.**

Make any changes that you require.

4. **Click Save. If you decide that no changes are necessary, click Close.**

5. **Select the components of the order that you want to update and click Update.**

The Batch Supplier window appears, showing the details of your purchase invoice.

6. **Match the actual invoice received from your supplier with the details shown on the Batch Supplier window.**

You need to add the supplier's invoice number in the Ex Ref field or the Details field. You also need to enter your sequential number for your purchase invoice in the Ref field. You can overtype the order number that automatically pulls through in the Ref field.

When you file your purchase invoices, you can attach a copy of the printed order to the back of the invoice.

7. **To update the purchase ledger and create an invoice from the details, click Save.**

The Purchase Order list now shows a *Y* in the Posted column for the invoice you just updated.

Deleting, Cancelling and Un-Cancelling Orders

Sometimes you need to delete or cancel an order. Sage knows the realities of the business world and accommodates them. And sometimes, you think that you need to cancel a purchase order only to find out that you need it after all. Sage accommodates these human foibles as well.

Deleting

You can delete purchase orders from the Purchase Order list. However, if you try to delete an order that's neither complete nor cancelled, Sage issues a warning message asking if you really want to delete this.

Note that when Sage deletes a purchase order, it also deletes any associated goods received notes, so if you need to keep copies of GRNs, take copies prior to deleting the orders.

After you delete the purchase orders, you can use the Compress Files facility in File Maintenance to remove deleted orders from the data files and make available the unused disk space.

Before you delete a purchase order, a wise move is to take a backup (in case things go pear-shaped, and you need to restore a clean set of data)! Then you can select the order you want to delete from your Purchase Order List and click Delete at the bottom of the screen. A confirmation box appears asking you to confirm that you want to delete the items high-lighted. Click Yes to continue or No to halt the process.

Cancelling

With Sage, you have the ability to cancel orders. This is easily done by selecting the appropriate order from your Purchase Order List, and by then clicking Amend. The Amend Deliveries window appears, showing the details of the order, with one line per product. You can then click Off Order.

Clicking the Off Order button cancels the whole order. If you want to cancel one line from an order, choose the New/Edit icon from the Purchase Order List window and delete the required row from the order by using the F8 key.

The status of the PO needs to be *on order* before you can cancel it. Otherwise, when you click Amend, the Off Order button isn't available.

Putting a cancelled order back on order

If you change your mind and decide that a previously can-
celled order needs reinstating, select the order from your
Purchase Order List, and click Amend. If you click Order
in the Amend Deliveries window the button changes to Off
Order. You can exit the Amend Deliveries window by clicking
Close. The status of the order will now show as *on order.*

Chapter 12

Keeping Track of Your Products

· ·

In This Chapter

▶ Recording a stocktake

▶ Building a Bill of Materials

▶ Processing stock returns

▶ Assigning stock

· ·

A lot of money is often tied up in stock, and having proper control over your stock procedures makes good business sense. In this chapter, I give you the tools to do this.

I cover recording a stocktake, which you can do with any version of Sage, in the first section of this chapter; I then explore the added features available only in Sage Plus and Professional versions.

Taking Stock

Every business should undertake a stocktake periodically – once a year at the very least – so that the year-end accounts show an accurate stock position.

To record a stocktake using Sage, follow these steps:

1. **From the navigation bar, click Products.**

   Ensure that the screen is displaying the Products view and not the Products dashboard (which shows graphs). Use the Change View button to switch the display if necessary.

2. **Select the products for which you want to do a stock-take. Click Stk Take to display the Stocktake window, which shows the product lines you selected.**

   Figure 12-1 shows a sample Stocktake window.

Product Code	Details	Date	Ref	Actual	Cost Price	In stock	Adjustment
CARD-ANNIV25 ☑	25th Wedding Anni...	27/07/2008	STK TAKE	100.00	0.50	100.00	0.00
CARD-GW	Get Well Soon Card	27/07/2008	STK TAKE	125.00	0.50	125.00	0.00
CARD-HB	Card - Happy Birthday	27/07/2008	STK TAKE	1170.00	0.50	1170.00	0.00
PAPERGOLD	A4 Sheets of Gold c...	27/07/2008	STK TAKE	50.00	0.25	50.00	0.00
PAPERHAND	A4 handmade paper...	27/07/2008	STK TAKE	100.00	0.50	100.00	0.00
PAPERSILVER	A4 sheet of silver co...	27/07/2008	STK TAKE	50.00	0.25	50.00	0.00

Figure 12-1: A Stocktake window for Jingles.

3. **Print the stocktake information and use it as the basis of your stocktake.**

   As you go around counting the items, tick them off on the list and note any stock adjustments that you need to make.

4. **Make adjustments in Sage according to the stocktake information.**

   If you find differences in the quantity of stock items, amend the Actual column, which in turn generates a figure in the Adjustment column – a positive number if the quantity of stock is more than the Actual column shows, and a negative number if the stock is less.

5. **To post the new stock levels, click Save. If you don't want to record your entries, click Discard.**

   You can memorise the changes prior to posting by clicking Memorise and entering a file name where you want to save the information before clicking Save. To open that file at a later time, click Recall and select the appropriate file.

Adjusting stock levels

Apart from the automatic changes made when you generate sales or purchase orders, Sage helps you to adjust stock levels. For example, you may need to return some goods to stock without generating a credit note – a *stock in* movement – or record the fact that you sent some stock out to potential customers as samples – a *stock out* movement. As you're not processing credit notes or sales orders, you need to change the stock numbers manually to reflect the movement in stock.

To make a stock adjustment, you select the product that you want to make an adjustment to from the Product module. Click the In icon to put stock back into your stores, or click Out to remove items. The Stock Adjustment In/Out window appears, and you just enter the adjustment details, using one line per product. Entering a reason for the adjustment in the Reference column is a good idea – you have 30 spaces to enter a description. To save the details you've entered, click Save. The stock is automatically adjusted.

If you want to check on stock, simply highlight the product and click the Activity icon. You can see a history of all stock movements for that product item.

Checking stock activity

You can look at a product's activity and view stock movements. The Activity screen records all movement of stock in and out and written off. As well as stock movements, you can also use the Activity screen to view the precise sales orders and purchase orders responsible for the goods in and out. Click the little grey and white arrow next to the Goods In/Out description, and Sage shows you the order and its current status.

To check product activity, all you need to do is select the product that you want to view, click Activity and the Activity screen opens, showing all movements of stock. You can print a list of activities or click Close to close this screen. You'll then return to the Products list.

Using the stock shortfall facility

You can use the Shortfall facility to see if your stock levels have fallen below the reorder levels you set in your product records. If you use Accounts Professional, you can automatically create a purchase order for those items.

Figure 12-2 shows a Shortfall report, generated because the reorder level for 25th Anniversary cards is set at 125 units and the cards in stock have fallen below that level. Clicking the

Create Order button at the bottom right of that screen produces a purchase order for the supplier of those cards.

Figure 12-2: In Accounts Professional you can generate a purchase order
from a Shortfall report.

If you have a number of products on your shortfall list, sort
the list into supplier order by clicking the top of the Supplier
column. Print the list, so you can methodically place orders
with each supplier.

If you always buy the same products from the same suppliers, you can enter the supplier reference in the appropriate
field within the product record, which makes it even easier to
place orders. You simply select all the products that have the
same supplier reference and place a bulk order. The Create
Order button available in Accounts Professional lets you do
this automatically.

To create a product shortfall list, click the Swap button at
the bottom of the screen. All your product records are highlighted. Then click the Shortfall icon. The Product Shortfall
Generator window opens, showing a list of all items that have
fallen below the reorder level. You can click Print List to
obtain a copy of these items.

Understanding a Bill of Materials

A *bill of materials (BOM)* is best described as a list of products used to make up another product – the component parts
of the main product.

You set up each component as a separate product record and link them all together with a BOM; the various levels of components get different names. To help you keep everything straight, look at the following example. I use a Magic Party product that the fictional card shop Jingles offers.

The *product assembly,* or the list of components that make up a product – in this case, a Jingles Magic Party – includes the following elements:

- ✔ A magician
- ✔ A box of tricks
- ✔ Wizard-themed party dishes pack

Each of these three items is a *subassembly* of the product assembly – it may be an individual component (such as the magician) or a group of components that together form the main product assembly, for example, the box of tricks below.

The box of tricks subassembly contains the following *components,* which are the individual items that form assemblies when grouped together:

- ✔ 1 pack of cards
- ✔ 6 feather dusters
- ✔ 6 silk scarves
- ✔ 1 box of party poppers
- ✔ 1 pack of blow-up balloons

The BOM shows the levels of components and subassemblies, and the number of assemblies or subassemblies to which each component belongs – known as the *link.*

Creating a bill of materials

Jeanette, Jingles' owner, needs to create a product record for each subassembly – and each of their components. Fortunately for her, creating a bill of materials is a relatively simple process – a bit like making a shopping list. You essentially create a new product, the BOM, from other products that you hold in stock.

You need to create a product record for the new product, and then use the BOM tab on the product record to build up the list of products required to make it!

To set up a bill of materials:

1. **From Products, choose the product record that you want to create a BOM for and click Record.**

   This opens up the Product Record screen.

2. **Click the BOM tab on the top of the screen.**

   The BOM information table appears, which is blank to start with.

3. **Enter the product code and quantity required of each item needed for the BOM.**

   Figure 12-3 shows the BOM for the Magic Party's components, which include:

   • **Product code:** Select the product items required for your main product.

   In the case of this Magic Party, the items include a box of tricks, a magician and a party dishes pack.

   • **Assembly level:** This field shows how many levels of components and subassemblies are below this component. Sage automatically generates this number.

   • **Link level:** This is the number of assemblies or subassemblies to which this component belongs. Each product can be a component of more than one assembly or subassembly.

   Sage automatically creates a link count for each component on the BOM.

   • **Available to make up:** This field shows the number of units that can be made with the current stock levels.

Figure 12-3: Jeanette has created a BOM for a Magic Party.

Before Jeanette sets up a BOM for the Magic Party, she needs to decide what the subcomponents are. She decides upon a magician, a box of tricks and a party dishes pack. At this point, she needs to set up a product record for each of these subcomponents before she can select them for her Magic Party BOM. Whilst she is setting up her box of tricks product record, she can click the BOM tab and select the list of products required to make a box of tricks. She also needs to do the same exercise for the party dishes product record and list the component parts on the BOM tab.

After the subassemblies are set up, Jeanette can click her BOM tab for the Magic Party and select the relevant subassemblies. As soon as she enters Box of Tricks, the assembly level becomes *1* rather than *0*. The number one indicates that Box of Tricks is a subassembly of the main assembly. The magician, however, remains as assembly level zero, because there are no further subcomponents.

Checking stock availability for a BOM

You can use the Check BOM option to see if you have enough stock available to assemble the main product. Follow these steps:

1. **From the Product module task pane, click Check BOM.**

   The Check Stock Make Up window appears.

2. **From the Product Code dropdown list, select the code of the assembly that you want to check.**

   The description of the assembly appears in a text box. You can't edit this information.

3. **In the Quantity box, select the number of assemblies you want to make and click Check.**

   If you don't have enough of an item of stock, a message appears saying how many assemblies you're short of. Click OK to find out what items you need to order. If you have enough components in stock, a confirmation message appears saying that.

You can create a purchase order automatically by selecting the items you're short of and clicking Create Order.

4. To print a Component Availability report, click Print.

Figure 12-4 shows the component parts required for a Magic Party. Sage says that there are no components in stock and gives a list of products that Jeanette needs to order.

The Check BOM screen only shows product items, not service items, so if a BOM includes a service as well as products, you need to deal with the service element separately.

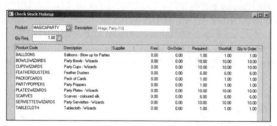

Figure 12-4: Checking component parts for a Magic Party.

Transferring stock for a BOM

You use the Product Transfer function to increase the quantity of product assemblies in stock by using components currently in stock.

In the Jingles example, to get a Magic Party into stock, Jeanette needs to transfer its components and the party itself into stock.

When you use the Product Transfer facility, Sage automatically calculates the cost of the product assembly by adding together the cost of the component parts.

To complete a product transfer:

1. From Products, click Transfer.

The Product Transfer screen appears.

2. **Insert the details for each transfer in the lines provided, using one line per transfer.**

   Each transfer must involve a product assembly. So in the example, Jeanette selects a Magic Party, a box of tricks and party dishes. She enters a quantity of *1* and Sage transfers the necessary component parts into those items of stock, as shown in Figure 12-5.

Product Code	Details	Date	Ref.	Quantity	In stock	On order	Allocated
MAGICAPARTY	Magic Party (10)	03/08/2008		1.00	0.00	0.00	0.00
BOXOFTRICKS	Box of Tricks	03/08/2008		1.00	0.00	0.00	0.00
PARTYDISHESWI...	Party Dishes - bowls, pla...	03/08/2008		1.00	0.00	0.00	0.00
		/ /		0.00	0.00	0.00	0.00

Figure 12-5: Transferring stock to BOMs.

3. **As soon as you're happy with the information, you can click Save or Discard to cancel. Click Close to exit the Product Transfer screen.**

When you carry out a stock transfer, Sage carries out the following postings:

✔ Increases the in-stock quantity of the finished product by the quantity entered. This transaction is recorded as a *Movement In (MI)* on the product activity file.

✔ Reduces the in-stock quantity of each individual component type. The transfer is recorded as a *Movement Out (MO)*.

✔ Updates the product activity file with each transfer made.

✔ Updates the cost price of the finished product in the product record.

Processing Stock Returns

You may have stock returned for a variety of reasons – the customer just didn't like it (their bad taste is their problem!), the item didn't fit, or didn't fit their needs, or was the wrong colour, size or whatever. When this happens, you have to adjust your stock levels. You can adjust your stock levels by issuing a credit note and updating the system (which in turn updates the stock levels) or by making an *adjustment in* to stock.

The Stock Return option isn't available if you selected the product code as a non-stock or service item. Refer to Chapter 3 for more information.

If the returned items are damaged or faulty, you use a different method to process the stock return to accommodate the ultimate destination of the defective goods:

- ✔ **Damaged goods returned to you (damages in):** Because you can't just add faulty items back into your stock and sell them again, you create a record of the stock return that doesn't increase the in-stock quantity.

- ✔ **Damaged goods you're returning to your supplier (damages out):** Again, as the goods are being returned for repair or replacement, you don't update the quantity in stock, sales value or sales quantity figures.

- ✔ **Write off:** Use this option if you need to *write off* the stock, which means determining that it has no value and you can't sell it. Sage makes an adjustment to the stock levels in the same way that an adjustment out does.

    At least once a year, you have to value your stock for accounts purposes. Any written off stock reduces the value of the stock in the accounts. You can obtain a Product Writeoff Details report from the Product Reports window, in a subsection of Product Damage and Writeoff Reports. This report can help you identify the value of stock to be written off in the accounts. I advise talking to your accountant about processing this type of adjustment in your accounts.

You can record a stock return by selecting the product you want to record a return for and clicking on the Returns icon in the Products toolbar. The Stock Return window appears and you can enter the stock return details as necessary. To post the stock return, click Save.

Allocating Stock

If you run Plus or Professional versions of Sage, you can manually allocate stock for general use or project use and allocate it to a project by way of a purchase order. Both manual and purchase order stock allocations affect the committed costs of a project. *Committed costs* are costs allocated to a project. Committed costs are not formally charged to a project until the stock allocated to a project is issued. See the upcoming 'Issuing allocated stock' section.

When you record a stock allocation, you can't allot more than the amount of available stock, called *free stock,* unless you set your program to allow negative stock. After you assign stock, it's no longer free and can't be used for other sales orders.

To allocate stock, follow these steps:

1. **From Products, click the Allocate icon.**

   The Allocation window appears, with the Allocate Stock option highlighted.

2. **Click OK.**

   The Stock Allocation window appears.

3. **From the Stock Allocation window, enter the stock allocation details.**

   Using the dropdown arrows, enter the product code, the project reference and the cost code, if required. Figure 12-6 shows allocation information for Jingles. Jeanette has decided to allocate 27 sheets of handmade A4 paper to an order. Sage has calculated that 100 sheets are available.

   Sage automatically shows the amount of free stock, but you need to enter the quantity of stock you want to allocate.

Product Code	Details	Date	Ref.	Project Ref	Cost Code	Qty to Allocate	Free Stock	On order
PAPERHAND	A4 handmade paper	04/08/2008				27.00	100.00	0.00
		/ /				0.00	0.00	0.00

Figure 12-6: Jeanette decides to allocate some handmade paper to a customer's order.

4. **To print a copy of the stock information you've entered, click Print List.**

5. **To save the allocation, click Save. If you don't want to save the information, click Discard. Click Close to return to the Products window.**

You can view how much stock is allocated by looking at the bottom left corner of the product record, as shown in Figure 12-7. The record shows how much of that item is in stock, how much of it is allocated and how much is free stock.

Figure 12-7: The product record after stock is allocated.

Changing stock allocation

You can amend any previous allocations you made to stock by selecting the product and clicking Make Allocations on the Task pane (or clicking the Allocate icon). The Allocation window appears and you should select View/Amend Allocations and click OK. Select the product you want to amend or delete by using the dropdown arrow and clicking OK. Change the allocated quantity by overtyping. You can only change the quantity.

Pressing **0** (zero) removes a product allocation. By removing a product allocation, you increase the amount of free stock available for that product and reduce the allocated amount. For example, you may want to do this if a big order came in for a valued customer and you needed to ship it quickly. You can decide to take stock that had been previously allocated to another customer and reallocate it to your priority order.

To save the details of the stock allocation, click Save. If you want to clear the allocation, click Discard.

If any of the stock was allocated to projects, the costs become committed to the project and you can view this stock on a committed costs report.

Issuing allocated stock

After stock has been allocated, it needs to be issued. By issuing stock, you update your stock records and stock allocation records. When issuing an allocation associated with a project, the value of the issued stock is applied to the cost of the project. In other words, Sage converts *committed costs* to *actual costs* for the project.

To issue stock, click Make Allocations from the Task pane or click the Allocate icon. Click Issue Allocations and then click OK. The Issue Allocations window opens, as shown in Figure 12-8. You can use the dropdown arrow to select the product that you want to issue. Enter the quantity of stock you want to issue and click Save. Alternatively, you can click Issue All.

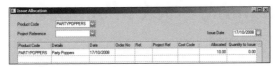

Figure 12-8: Issuing allocated stock.

The product must be allocated before it can be issued (see the preceding section). You can choose to issue less than the whole quantity of stock. Only the stock you choose to issue is allocated and charged to the project; the balance remains as committed stock.

You need to be aware of the following rules when issuing allocated stock:

✔ When issuing stock to a project, you must ensure that the status of the project allows postings.

✔ You can't change the details of a stock allocation, such as the project reference or cost codes, during a stock issue. You can only change the stock quantity.

✔ A stock issue can't exceed the allocation amount, regardless of the negative stock setting.

Chapter 13

Managing Projects

· ·

In This Chapter

▶ Assigning status and costs to a project

▶ Managing project resources

▶ Recording project costs, including purchase order processing

▶ Analysing project costs

▶ Charging project costs to your customers

▶ Completing a project

· ·

Sage's Project Costing tool, available to users of Accounts Plus and Accounts Professional, enables businesses large and small to successfully manage a project.

With Sage, you can track costs and ensure that you capture every expenditure associated with a project. You can then charge the client a fee that produces a profit for your company. You can evaluate future projects more accurately and target your business towards more profitable ventures.

Appointing a Project's Status and Costs

Project status helps you track a project's progress. You can set the status to allow or disallow postings. Sage has five status categories for you to use according to where the project is in its life cycle, and each status has its own rules as to whether you can make postings to it or not.

Assigning status

Your project is assigned one of five default status categories. If it works really hard and attracts the right kind of people, it can change status . . . oh, sorry, my mistake, knowing the right people has nothing to do with it – a project status changes according to the stage it's in. In any case, the default status categories are:

 ✔ **Active:** This status indicates that a project is open and ongoing. You can make postings to the project, but you can't delete the record.

 ✔ **Snag:** Although completed, the project remains open so that you can still make final postings. You can't delete the record.

 ✔ **Completed:** The job is closed and you can't post to the project. You can delete the record if you want to.

 ✔ **Suspend:** The project has been suspended. You can't post to the project or delete the record. This status usually indicates a problem with the project.

 ✔ **Initial:** The project is at a pre-acceptance stage. Although you can make postings to the record, you can't delete it. You can use this status for very new projects that are just getting off the ground.

You can access the Configuration Editor and change the names of the status categories to ones that suit your business better. See the 'Changing status and costs' section later in this chapter.

Looking at costs – types and codes

You give each project a project reference and use that reference when recording costs to the project by using cost types and cost codes:

 ✔ **Cost type:** A label that describes an activity or resource. Labour and materials are examples of cost types.

 A cost type on its own is meaningless – it must be associated with a cost code.

The default cost type is *other*. This *other* cost type is linked to the default cost codes in the next point.

 ↙ **Cost code:** A *cost code* is a way to further differentiate cost types. For example, you can further divide the cost type *labour* into plumbers, carpenters, bricklayers and so on. You can create the cost code yourself, according to the needs of your business. You have just eight characters to name your cost codes, but you don't have to use all eight, so if you can get by with four characters, shorter is better. The default cost codes are labour (LAB1), materials (MAT1), overheads (OHD1) and mixed (MIX1).

A cost type can link to many cost codes, but a cost code can link to only one cost type.

You can view cost types and cost codes in the Configuration Editor, as shown in Figure 13-1.

You can set up budgets for a project against each cost code. When you apply costs to a project, it's the cost *code* that records the charge, not the cost *type*. For example, when entering a purchase invoice, you have a column for the project reference and then one for the cost code. There is no cost type column; instead, the cost codes are linked to the cost types in the Configuration Editor.

Changing status and costs

If you're using the default status set, the only time you want to change the status of the project is when it gets to a different stage in its lifecycle. For example, all projects start at the default status of *Active,* but when that project is complete, you no longer want to accept costs against that project. You need to change the status, as outlined in the last section in this chapter, 'Completing Your Project'. However, you can also change the default project status names to better describe your business needs. This section is all about how to make these changes. You can make the same name changes to the cost types and cost codes, so if you want to know how to personalise them, read on.

You can amend the project status, cost code or cost type by using the Configuration Editor window, which you access via Settings on the main toolbar. The Project Costing tab (shown in Figure 13-1) in this window enables you to amend the project status, cost type and or cost codes, which you can do by clicking the Edit button for the relevant section and changing the necessary details. For example, if you want to edit the cost codes, click Edit in the cost code section. The Edit Cost Code window appears, and you change the description or cost type and then click OK. You must click the Apply button – which greys out when you click Yes – to use this configuration on your accounts data. After clicking Close the second time, you return to the Welcome screen.

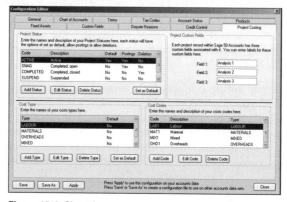

Figure 13-1: Changing your status, cost types and cost codes with the Configuration Editor.

You can edit and apply your own project status names, using titles that may be more meaningful to your business.

Managing Project Resources

To undertake work on a project, you need manpower, resources and equipment. Plant and machinery, computer equipment and people cost money, and you need to apply these costs to the project.

The term *resource* applies to any cost applied to a project. For example, you apply people costs via a timesheet. You can use the timesheet to apply labour costs to a project. Machinery has some sort of hire charge or other cost associated with it, which you can also apply to the project.

When you come to record a project charge, you select the type of resource used. You can use the resource information to calculate a total cost for the charge, but you can override this as the charge is recorded.

Creating or amending a resource

You can create as many resources as you want, but each one must have a unique reference.

You create or amend a resource by clicking Manage Resources in the Task pane. The Resources box opens and you click Add (for a new resource). To edit a resource, click Edit. If you're adding a new resource, you must give it a unique reference number, a name, a unit of measure (such as *hour*), a cost rate and a cost code (use the dropdown arrow). Click OK when you've added your details and your newly created or amended resource will appear in the Resources box.

When editing, you can't change a resource's reference number. You can change the name, the unit of measure, cost rate and cost code – but not the reference.

Deleting a resource

You can easily delete a resource that is no longer required by clicking Resources, highlighting the resource you want to delete and clicking Delete. A confirmation message appears. Click Yes to delete or No to return to the Resources window.

Tracking Project Costs

You can record costs or charges against a specific project as soon as they're incurred. For example, you can apply timesheets to a specific project when they're turned in. The following sections outline the mechanisms of applying costs – project charges, invoices, bank payments and stock issues – to both the accounts and projects.

To be able to apply costs to a project, the project must be set up to allow postings. Refer to the section 'Appointing a Project's Status and Costs' earlier in this chapter to find out about allowing postings.

Sharing out project charges

A project charge applies a cost to the project but doesn't charge the nominal ledger and therefore doesn't affect the accounts. This may sound a bit odd, but let me give you an example: labour costs go through the accounts by way of wages journals, which directly affect the accounts. But you can't post to Projects directly from a journal. So at a later stage, you need to allocate the applicable labour costs directly to the project by way of a project charge.

The types of project charges you can make include:

- ✔ **Labour charges:** You can take these from the rates and hours entered on timesheets.

- ✔ **Costs:** You can include costs that don't affect your stock, such as costs involving non-stock items or service items. You can't issue non-stock items to a project, so the only way to post a charge to the project for items of this nature is to process a project charge. You can only charge service items to a project this way. (Non-stock and service items are discussed in Chapter 3.)

- ✔ **Adjustments or corrections:** You can incorporate amendments to other costs for the project. For example, if you post an invoice to the wrong project, you can do a credit from the project without having to reverse the invoice. You can then put the appropriate charge through to the correct project.

Project charges are shown as transaction type CD (costing debits) in Sage, but you can also issue a cost credit (CC) if you need to make an adjustment to the project cost.

To record a *project only* cost or credit (the *only* indicates that you're only charging amounts to the project, not affecting your nominal ledger), follow these steps:

1. **From the Projects window, select the project for which you want to process a charge.**

2. **From the Projects toolbar, click Charge (or Credit if you need to credit the project).**

   The Project Charge or Project Credit window appears.

3. **Enter the details of the charge or credit in the boxes provided, using one line per charge.**

   You must enter a cost code for the cost. If you don't, Sage shows an error message when you try to save the cost.

   If you select a resource for the charge or credit, Sage automatically fills in the rate and cost code as the default rate from when you entered it on the resource list. You can overwrite this rate if you require.

   When you enter the quantity, the program automatically calculates the total cost and displays it in the Total Cost column.

4. **To save your entries, click Save. Click Discard to exit without saving.**

5. **Click Close to return to the Projects window.**

Figure 13-2 shows a charge for the costs of hiring Claris the Clown for the Fun Day project. Claris has been set up as a resource and given a cost code of LAB1. The Fun Day project is allotted the costs of the number of hours that Claris will work.

Figure 13-2: Applying a project charge to a project – Claris the Clown is a labour charge to the Fun Day project.

Issuing stock to a project

You often use stock on a project, and sometimes you don't use all of it. You can use the Products module to allocate stock to a project and put returned or unused products back into stock. These stock postings are shown as Adjustments In (AI) or Adjustments Out (AO) on the Product Activity screen.

You can find details about allotting stock in Chapter 12. Just remember to select a project reference and ensure that the project status allows postings.

When you allocate stock to a project, that stock is set aside for the use of that project. The cost of the stock becomes a *committed cost* to the project, but it only becomes an *actual cost* to the project when the stock is issued.

Sage uses a *first in first out (FIFO)* method of allocating stock, meaning it uses the oldest stock first. If you order stock specifically for a project and get a special price for it, you have to make a price adjustment to assign the correct price to the stock allocated to the project. Otherwise, Sage uses the stock price of the oldest stock first, which may be different from the price you paid.

Use the Products module to issue the stock, which then shows up in your project reports. (See the 'Integrating POP with project costing' section later in this chapter for more information.)

Figure 13-3 shows the issue of party poppers stock to the Fun Day project. The stock shows as an adjustment out of stock and against the project.

Product Code	Details	Date	Order No	Ref.	Project Ref	Cost Code	Allocated	Quantity to Issue
PARTYPOPPERS	Party Poppers	10/08/2008			FUNDAY	MAT1	5.00	5.00

Product Code: PARTYPOPPERS
Project Reference: FUNDAY
Issue Date: 10/08/2008

Figure 13-3: Party popper stock issued to the Fun Day project.

Stock issues are a cost to the project. Usually, when stock leaves your hands, you invoice a customer, the customer pays the invoice and money subsequently flows back into the business. When you allocate stock to a project, you don't get paid for it immediately or directly.

You can use the Clear Stock option as part of your month-end or year-end routine. This option involves removing stock transactions from your product activity record, up to and including a specified date. Note that any project active at the point you clear your stock still holds the details of all the transactions showing in its product activity, so you can maintain a complete history for that project.

Counting costs from a supplier invoice

You can post purchase invoices (PI), purchase credit notes (PC) and bank payments (BP) to a project. By doing so, you update your accounts with the cost and also link the cost to your project. (To see how to post a supplier invoice, refer to Chapter 7.) Just remember to enter the project reference in the Project Reference column and enter a valid cost code in the Cost Code column.

When you post an invoice to a project, you post a value to the project, but not a quantity. The Batch Entry screen for posting invoices doesn't have a quantity column – it just registers an amount. If you need to post quantities of an item to a project, post the invoice without a project reference, and then post a separate project charge to the project.

You can apply costs using bank payments. When making a bank payment, select a project reference and a cost code. That cost is then applied to the project. (For details on how to process a bank payment, refer to Chapter 8.)

Integrating POP with project costing

As Sage is an integrated system, you can link purchase order processing (POP) and projects. The project is updated at various points of the purchase-order life cycle:

- ✔ **Creating an order:** At the time of creating an order, give a project reference and enter a cost code.

- ✔ **On order:** After you place the goods on order, those costs are *committed* to the project, meaning that the value of those goods and services is applied to that project.

- ✔ **Goods received:** After you receive the goods, you can automatically allocate them to stock and then allocate that stock to the project. You can see that the stock has been allocated to the project by clicking the product record and looking at the Stock Allocated box in the lower left corner of the record.

✔ **Stock issued:** After the stock is issued, the amount of allocated stock reduces; *actual costs* are applied to the project and committed costs are reduced. The transaction is shown as an AO (adjustment out of stock) transaction type and shows the project reference and cost code associated with that transaction.

You can look at the Activity tab of the project record to see the transaction.

✔ **Invoice:** For stock items, you apply the actual cost to the project at the point the stock is issued. When stock is issued to a project, the costs convert from *committed* to *actual costs.* You can update the invoice at a later point to ensure that the accounts and supplier ledger have been updated.

You must manually issue the stock to the project by going into the Products module. The purchase order only allocates stock to your project and labels it a committed cost. When you formally issue the stock to the project, the committed costs change to actual costs.

When you update your purchase order, notice that in the Batch Supplier Invoice screen, the project reference and cost code are blank. Do *not* re-enter the project reference and cost code. If you enter the project reference on the Batch Supplier Invoice screen, you post the actual costs for a second time, thus double-counting. Click Save instead. Sage flashes up a warning message about double-counting. Click Yes to continue. You're then returned to the Purchase Order Processing window.

For non-stock items, the actual cost to the project is applied when you generate and update the invoice. When you produce a purchase order for these items, enter the project reference and cost code on the Batch Supplier screen, as it allows you to post the actual costs to the project. When you click Save, a warning message appears, saying:

```
If you have already entered a project reference
for these items on the purchase order, they will
automatically become a realised cost when the
stock is issued. You may be double-counting for
these items. Are you sure you want to continue?
```

Click Yes. As you've created a service invoice, not a stock invoice, you're not issuing any stock and therefore can't be double-counting.

 You can review the value of both committed costs and actual costs by looking at the Analysis tab of the relevant project record.

Analysing Project Costs

Sage has several features that help you to track your projects and analyse your costs and revenues. Tracking and analysing gives you the ability to respond to customer enquiries about the projects.

Looking at the project's activity

When you're analysing a project, the first thing you may want to do is look at the Project Activity screen. This screen shows you all the transactions with a specific project reference. You can also filter the transactions by type with the Custom Range button, as explained in the following steps:

1. **From Projects, click the Activity tab or select the specific project and click Activity.**

   The transaction information for the project appears.

   If the project you select is a multi-level project, tick the Include Rolled Up Transactions check box to show all the transactions for all the projects linked with the one you're viewing.

2. **Filter the transactions by clicking the dropdown arrow next to the Show field to select specific calendar months or by clicking the Custom Range button.**

   Clicking the Custom Range option opens up an Activity Range window. You can view the project activity by specific transaction types or display all transactions.

 Sage remembers the filter that you used, so the next time you view the activity, Sage applies the same filter until you change it.

You can look at the transactions that are recorded against a project. These transactions may include the following types:

- ✔ **CD:** A project charge (costing debit).

- ✔ **CC:** A project credit (costing credit).

- ✔ **AO:** A stock adjustment out of stock into the project.

- ✔ **AI:** A stock adjustment out of the project back into stock.

- ✔ **PI:** A purchase invoice, which you can generate from a purchase order if you have Accounts Professional.

- ✔ **PC:** A purchase credit note may be issued to the project.

- ✔ **BP:** A bank payment.

- ✔ **SI:** A sales invoice is issued to charge the customer, as part of the project billing process.

- ✔ **SC:** A credit note can be issued to the customer in respect of adjustments to the project billing process.

Stock allocations aren't displayed as part of the project activity.

As well as looking at the specific project record, you can also check the customer record associated with the project. Just access the Projects tab from the customer record to view a list of every project associated with that customer. Figure 13-4 shows the customer record for Any Town Parish Council and the Fun Day project associated with it. The record shows the price quoted for the project and the costs billed to date.

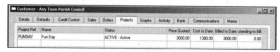

Figure 13-4: Showing a project associated with a customer – viewed from the Projects tab of the customer's record.

Comparing costs to budget

Comparing actual costs of a project against a budget gives you an indication of how well the project is being managed. Costs at or below budget give a good indication of a well-managed project. Costs starting to exceed the budget indicate that the project is not going as planned and that costs need to be controlled. Each aspect of the project needs investigating to see why costs are exceeding budget.

To assign a budget, select the project you require, click Record and then click the Budgets tab. The budget information shows all cost codes currently set up in Sage 50 Accounts. Select the Budget column for each labour cost and enter a figure. You can then save your entries.

You've now successfully applied budgets to your project.

To see how the project costs compare to the budget, click the Analysis tab on the project record. You can view a summary of actual costs, budgeted costs and committed costs here.

You can run many reports to check the progress of your project. You can run reports showing committed costs for each project; cost transactions by cost code; checking stock issued for a project and a number of day book reports allowing you to see postings to the project by various transactions types. To print a report, simply click Reports from Projects and select whichever report you require from the array of reports available.

Charging Your Customers for a Project

Ultimately, you need to charge your customers for work carried out on your project. If the project is large, you may want to do this on a continual basis. If the project is a small one-day project, as in the Jingles Fun Day example, then you invoice at the end of the project.

Project costing doesn't automatically bill your customers, but the Analysis tab of the project record helps you calculate how much to charge them. You can see how much you've billed a customer already or how much you've quoted a customer and therefore what is outstanding. Sage provides a variety of project-costing reports that can help you decide how much to charge your customer.

After you know how much you're going to charge, you can invoice your customer in a number of ways:

✔ Issue a service invoice, showing details of work carried out.

✔ Issue a product invoice, using special product code S3 (only if you have Accounts Professional). This product code allows you to issue service charges and product charges on the same invoice.

✔ Issue a product invoice, showing non-stock or service items. You can use this type of invoice if your business is service-based, but you use product records to keep track of your services or to produce price lists.

If you overcharge a customer for a project, you can credit your customer by raising a credit note. (Refer to Chapter 6 for how to raise product and service invoices.)

When you enter the invoice, you must ensure that you include the project reference and cost code. When the invoice is posted to the ledger, it updates the project activity information and the Analysis tab.

A number of reports provide you with the information necessary to produce an invoice based on time and materials used. This process isn't automated, so you need to produce your bills manually. Refer to Chapter 6 for details.

Completing Your Project

After the project has come to an end and you no longer have any invoices or transactions to post to it, you need to mark the project as being complete. Changing the status to *complete* ensures that no further postings can be made to it.

You can change the status of the project by highlighting the project you want to complete and clicking Record. This takes you to the Details tab where on the status line, use the dropdown arrow to select the status *complete*. You can then save your changes. You've now successfully completed your project.

If at some time in the future, you no longer need to view this project record and have no need for any further analysis of the project, you may delete the project. You can only do this if the project shows the status as being complete.

To delete a project, simply highlight the project you want to delete and click Delete.

Part IV
Running Monthly, Quarterly and Annual Routines

'Reading your accounts in the tea leaves
is not really very satisfactory, Miss Jones.'

In this part . . .

You need to perform certain routines regularly – some monthly, some quarterly and some at the end of the year. The chapters in this part look at the procedures that you need to carry out when you prepare monthly accounts and year-end reports.

The VAT return is a key quarterly deadline that VAT-registered businesses have to meet: I give you information on what to do in Chapter 16.

I also look at running monthly reports in Chapter 17.

Chapter 14

Reconciling Your Bank Accounts

● ●

In This Chapter

▶ Valuing the importance of bank reconciliations

▶ Reconciling your bank account

▶ Checking things out when things don't check out

▶ Clearing up items that haven't cleared

● ●

Do you like to know to the penny what's in your bank account? If so, then this is the chapter for you! Reconciling your bank accounts normally forms part of your monthly accounting routine. Running through the bank reconciliation process gives you a thorough review of your bank statements and is an opportunity to investigate any unusual or incorrect transactions. As a result, you're fully aware of the financial transactions flowing in and out of your bank accounts.

Recognising Reasons to Reconcile

Performing a bank reconciliation requires you to check that you've matched all the bank transactions in Sage against the entries on your bank statements. Ultimately, you should be able to tick off every item on your bank statement against a corresponding entry in Sage.

Most businesses have at least one current account, a deposit account and possibly a business credit card, as well as a petty cash tin. Each one needs to have statements of one sort or another. Sage assumes that you have all these accounts and provides default accounts for each one, which you can rename or add to as required. (Refer to Chapter 3 for how to amend accounts.) Additionally, Sage includes a Building Society account and Credit Card Receipts account as default accounts, as shown in Figure 14-1.

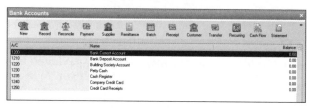

Figure 14-1: The bank accounts Sage assumes you to have.

You need to reconcile all your bank accounts to ensure the accuracy of the accounting records and of any reports run from the information. Reconciling all bank accounts is important, particularly if you're VAT registered, because in doing so you pick up all transactions that have VAT associated with them. Credit cards transactions in particular can attract a lot of VAT. If you don't reconcile credit card statements, you can miss VAT-liable transactions and render both the accounts and the VAT return incorrect.

When you set up your bank records, you're given the opportunity to determine whether you want the bank account to be a reconciling one or not. If you don't want to reconcile an account, simply click the bank record and put a tick in the No Bank Reconciliation box. However, use this feature with caution! Most bank accounts need to be reconciled to ensure accuracy of information.

Doing your bank reconciliations on a regular basis not only guarantees the accuracy of your information, but also gives you the ability to run meaningful reports that help you manage your business and enable you to make sensible decisions.

Getting Ready to Reconcile

The aim of a reconciliation is to match transactions in Sage with your bank statement, so the process is easier if you've entered as many transactions as possible prior to looking at the bank statement. Before starting a reconciliation, make sure that you've accomplished the following tasks:

> ✔ **Entered all the payments from your cheque stubs for the period you're reconciling.** Refer to Chapter 7 for a reminder on how to process supplier payments and Chapter 8 for all other payment types.
>
> ✔ **Entered the receipts from your paying-in book, up to and including the date to which you're reconciling**. Refer to Chapter 5 for help with processing customer receipts and Chapter 8 for recording other bank receipts.

Make sure that you enter the cheque numbers and payslip numbers in the Reference field so that you can easily identify those items on your statement.

Doing the Actual Reconciliation

You need your bank statements in front of you as you work through the reconciliation process, so have them at hand (where they should be if you prepared properly according to the tips I offer in the preceding section).

If you mark each item with a tick as you enter it onto Sage, you can then put a line through the tick or use a highlighter pen to indicate that you've reconciled that item. Make your mark visible, so that you can easily spot anything that hasn't been reconciled. Figure 14-2 shows an example of a bank statement with marks for items entered and reconciled in this way. The payments are all entered onto Sage and reconciled; the receipts have been entered, but aren't yet reconciled.

BISI BANK LTD
Statement Period ended 30.04.10

Account No: 51235467   Sortcode: 21.45.85

		Payments	Receipts	Balance
01.04.10	Account Opened			£0
01.04.10	100001		£2000✓	£2000
01.04.10	Cheque No 1	£100 ✗		£1900
15.04.10	Cheque No 2	£29.38 ✗		£1870.62
15.04.10	100002		£200 ✓	£2070.62
15.04.10	DD Denby DC	£120 ✗		£1950.62
30.04.10	balance carried forward			£1950.62

Figure 14-2: A bank statement with the different types of ticks.

To begin the reconciliation process, follow these steps:

1. **From the navigation bar, click Bank.**

   Make sure that your cursor is highlighting the bank account you want to reconcile. Sage defaults to account 1200, which is the Bank Current account, so move the cursor if necessary.

2. **Click Reconcile to bring up a statement summary, as shown in Figure 14-3.**

Figure 14-3: Statement summary for bank reconciliation.

3. **Enter the statement summary information.**

Your statement summary contains the following fields for you to fill in:

- **Statement reference:** Sage helpfully gives you a default reference, the first four digits being the bank account nominal code and the remaining reference being today's date. You can easily over-write this reference and use one that may be more meaningful to you. Giving your statement a refer-ence, allows Sage to archive the reconciliation into History. Archiving the statement means that you can pull up a copy of that bank reconciliation at any point in the future. The reference is used to name the PDF document created when archived.

- **Ending balance:** Enter the final balance shown on the bank statement for the period you're reconciling.

Most people reconcile to the end of the month, but I find it easier to reconcile a page at a time: you have fewer transactions to reconcile, which means fewer transactions to check back through in the event of an error (yes, errors happen to the best of us!). To reconcile by page, simply use the balance at the bottom of the statement page and reconcile each item on that single page.

- **Statement date:** Sage automatically defaults to today's date, so change this to the date of the bank statement you're reconciling.

- **Interest earned:** If there's any interest received on the bank statement, enter it here. Alternatively, you can enter any interest as an adjustment in Step 6.

- **Account charges:** Enter any bank charges on this screen, or enter an adjustment on the Bank Reconciliation screen in Step 4.

4. **Click OK to bring up the Bank Reconciliation screen, shown in Figure 14-4.**

If you click OK without changing any of the informa-tion on the statement summary, you still get the opportunity to change both the statement balance and date on the actual Reconciliation screen itself.

Figure 14-4: The Bank Reconciliation screen.

The screen is split into two parts. The top part shows all the transactions currently entered in Sage that need to be matched against the bank statement (up to and including the statement-end date, shown at the top of the screen). Items move to the bottom part of the screen after you match them against the bank statement. The bottom screen also shows any account charges or interest earned if you entered it on the statement summary, as well as showing you the last reconciled balance. If it's the first time a reconciliation has been performed, the last reconciled balance is zero. Otherwise, the balance from the previous reconciliation shows.

Sage only brings up transactions posted to the system up to the statement-end date that you enter on the Summary screen. In Figure 14-4, the end date is 30 June, so only items dated on or before that date appear. If you didn't specify a date on the Summary screen, Sage brings up *all* transactions posted to the system date, which is the current day's date, so you're looking at quite a few transactions!

To change the statement-end balance and the date whilst in the Bank Reconciliation screen, overtype the date and end balance at the top of the screen.

5. **Match items on Sage against the bank statement.**

   Match each item on your bank statement against the same item in the top part of the Bank Reconciliation screen. To do this, double-click the item in the top box or highlight it and click the Match Transaction button to the right of the screen. When you match an item, it moves to the bottom part of the screen and the values of the Matched Balance and the Difference boxes at the bottom right of the screen change accordingly.

   As you double-click each item in Sage, make a corresponding mark on the bank statement. If you ticked items on the statement, put a cross through the same tick or highlight the item. You can then identify anything not reconciled at the end.

   If you move a transaction to the bottom section in error, just double-click the transaction or highlight the transaction and click Unmatch Transaction, and it moves back to the unmatched items at the top.

   The three boxes at the bottom right of the screen keep track of the balance between the transactions you match and what your statement says. If everything agrees, the Difference box contains a zero.

6. **Click the Adjust button (above Difference at the bottom right of the screen) to make adjustments.**

   You may find that you missed inputting an entry that's on the bank statement. If you have Sage 50 2011, you can now make even more adjustments directly from the adjustment screen shown in Figure 14-5. New additions are supplier payments and customer receipts, as well as supplier and customer refunds.

   When you're happy that you have completed any adjustments, you can then move to step 7.

Figure 14-5: Adding an adjustment directly to your bank reconciliation.

7. **Save the reconciliation.**

Ideally, you work through the bank reconciliation until you've matched all your items from the bank statement. However, life isn't like that. Your phone may ring, or someone walks into your office to chat. Save the work you've done so far by clicking Save, near the bottom left of the screen, and then click OK.

When you're ready to continue reconciling, click the Reconcile icon. A pop-up screen asks whether you want to use the previously saved statement or discard it. Click the Use Saved button, and Sage takes you back to the point where you left off.

Clicking Discard Saved wipes out your previous work, and you have to start your reconciliation again.

8. **Reconcile your bank transactions.**

All your transactions match, and the Difference box reads zero, so click Reconcile on the bottom left of your screen. Sage saves your reconciled statement in a history file (using the reference you gave your reconciliation at the start of the reconciliation process). You can review it later if you need to.

To access archived reconciliations, click the Bank Reconcile button then click OK from the Statement Summary screen to open up the Reconciliation screen. Here, you can then click the View History button at the bottom of the screen. A list of PDF files appears, displaying your historical bank reconciliations.

Troubleshooting when Your Account Doesn't Reconcile

Hopefully, your accounts always reconcile. But, if they don't try these suggestions:

✔ See if every item on your bank statement has been ticked off. You may have missed something, which is easy to do when you have lots of transactions on a page.

✔ Make sure that all the items left on the top part of the screen haven't yet cleared the bank account. On a bank statement several pages long, you can easily overlook a transaction, especially if you're going through the statement page by page.

✔ As a last resort, check off each item again, perhaps this time circling the items on the bank statement to differentiate your markings. You may have entered and ticked the same entry twice. If you have, double-click the offending item in the matched section of the Bank Reconciliation screen to unmatch it. You then need to find the transaction number of that item and delete it.

After you make sure that your difference is zero, you're in a position to save or reconcile.

If you reconcile a transaction by mistake, you can fix it by going into File Maintenance, clicking Corrections and finding that transaction. Click Edit Item, uncheck the Bank Reconciled box and save the changes. Click Yes to confirm the changes. The next time you open the bank reconciliation, that transaction appears.

Rounding Up Stragglers

You may find that even though the Difference box is zero, you still have unmatched items in the top part of the screen. This is perfectly normal. It just means that you've entered cheques or receipts that haven't cleared the bank account and therefore don't show on the current bank statement. For example, if you're preparing accounts to the end of March, you need to ensure that you've entered all cheques up to and including 31 March. However, the 31 March bank statement may not include cheques you wrote on 31 March – or even 30 March or 29 March – because they haven't cleared your bank yet. Your cheque may still be sitting on your supplier's desk, waiting for someone to take it to the bank.

Cheques that show on Sage, but aren't yet on your bank statement, are known as *unpresented cheques*. You may also have an *outstanding lodgement* or two – a deposit paid in toward the end of the month that doesn't appear on your bank statement because it hasn't cleared the banking system.

At the year-end, your accountant needs to perform a traditional bank reconciliation and has to know what the outstanding cheques and lodgements are. You can print a list of unpresented cheques and outstanding lodgements at the end of any month. To do this, you click the Report icon within the Bank module, select Unreconciled Transaction Reports and then Unreconciled Payments or Unreconciled Receipts – or both, one after the other.

The traditional bank reconciliation, as shown in Figure 14-6, is often done only at the year-end.

Bank Reconciliation as at 30th June 2010	
	£
Balance per Bank Statement	1133.95
Less unpresented cheques	0.00
Add back outstanding lodgements	55.00
Balance per Cash book	1188.95

Figure 14-6: The bank reconciliation that your accountant likes to prepare.

Sage 50 2011 offers much clearer bank reconciliation reports, and enables you to print out retrospective bank reconciliation reports from the Reports icon within the Bank module. You can also print out the Bank Reconciliation screen whilst you're reconciling, which you might find useful.

Chapter 15

Running Your Monthly and Yearly Routines

*T*he nominal ledger lists all the nominal codes that your company uses. These nominal codes, when grouped together, form the record of your company's assets, liabilities, income and expenditure. They are grouped together in categories identified in your Chart of Accounts, which I talk about in Chapter 2.

Sage uses the accounting principle of *accrual accounting.* Accrual accounting isn't just about accruals (bizarre as it sounds!), but about recording sales and purchases when they occur, not when cash changes hands; you match revenue with expenditure. For example, if you're preparing the accounts for the month of June, you need to make sure that you enter all the sales invoices for June even if you haven't been paid for them yet. You also check that all the purchase invoices relating to June are posted, so that you get an accurate reporting position.

In this chapter, I show you how to run wizards and create journals by using the nominal codes to run the monthly routines and yearly routines. You need these routines to produce timely and accurate reports for management decision-making.

If you're not running Accounts Plus or Accounts Professional, you can't perform some of the steps outlined in this chapter. Instead of benefiting from the wizards, you have to manually process your accruals, prepayments and depreciation by using a nominal journal. If you're not happy dealing with journals, then leave this for your friendly accountant!

Adding Up Accruals

An *accrual* is an amount you know you owe for a product or service you've received, but for which you haven't yet received the invoice. An accrual occurs for items that you pay in arrears, such as telephone bills. To maintain an accurate set of accounts, you post an accrual into your nominal ledger by using the appropriate journals. These journals increase the costs to the business and create an accrual for the value of the outstanding invoice. The accrual is treated as a liability within the accounts as the business owes money. As soon as you receive the bill, you can reverse the accrual.

Charging a monthly amount for a service that's normally paid in arrears has a smoothing effect on company profits. For example, a £3,000 telephone bill that's paid quarterly is accrued in the accounts for the three months prior to receiving the bill, and a charge of £1,000 is put through the accounts each month. Otherwise, the first two months of the quarter show artificially high profits and the third month shows artificially low profits when the full cost of the telephone bill hits the Profit and Loss account in one go. Obviously, the cumulative effect over the three months is the same, but the monthly effect can make the difference between a profit and a loss for that company. So reviewing your accruals and prepayments (which I talk about in the next section) is important for monthly reporting purposes.

If you're confident with your double-entry bookkeeping, you can post a debit to the Cost accounts and a credit to the Accruals account. However, Sage likes to make things easy for you and provides a wizard you can use to set up adjustments for any invoices you're likely to pay in arrears.

To access the wizards from Company, click the Accruals icon to open up the Accruals window and click Wizard to open the Nominal Ledger Accruals wizard. You then need to select the code for which you want to set up an accrual, so just click Next and follow the instructions! A confirmation message appears saying that the accruals will be posted to the ledgers when you run the month-end option.

Alternatively, if you're happy with the accrual process and don't need to be guided step by step with your friendly wizard, you can set up your accrual manually by clicking the Accruals icon and manually entering all the accrual details. When you're happy with the information entered for your accruals, click Save. A confirmation message appears, saying that these details will be posted to Sage when the month-end option is run. The accrual now appears on the Accruals list.

Unfortunately, if you're using the basic Sage Accounts program, you have to complete a nominal journal for your accruals, as you don't have the luxury of getting Sage to work it out for you. For the telephone costs example, the double-entry is a debit to the cost code (telephone 7502) and a credit to default accrual code 2109.

Counting Out Prepayments

A *prepayment* is basically payment in advance for services you haven't completely received. For example, your business buys a year-long radio advertising programme for £12,000, which is invoiced in March. The invoice is entered in March for the full value of the advertising programme, which is clearly not right as most of this invoice relates to a future period of time. So you create a prepayment for the 11 months of advertisements to come.

Registering a prepayment has the effect of decreasing the cost code in the expenses and increasing the Prepayments account in the debtors ledger because you've paid in advance for services that haven't been supplied in their entirety (effectively, the supplier owes you).

You can set up prepayments in much the same way as accruals. If you want to use the wizard method, then from Company click Prepayments. The Prepayments window opens, where you click Wizard and follow the steps. As soon as you click Finish, the prepayment appears on the list of prepayments. Click Save, and a confirmation message appears, saying that

the payments will only be posted when you run the month-
end option. Click OK.

Alternatively, you can manually prepare a prepayment from
Company and then click prepayments, but instead of clicking
the wizard, simply enter the details directly onto the screen
manually. This method is quicker, as you're not clicking
through so many screens.

Again, if you're using plain Sage Accounts, your nominal journal double-entry is a debit to Prepayments and a credit to the
cost code.

Depreciating Fixed Assets

A *fixed asset* is an item likely to be held in the business for
more than 12 months. They're usually big and expensive
items that have a long useful life, such as machinery, land,
buildings, cars and so on.

Because fixed assets last so long, you can't charge the Profit
and Loss account with their full value. Instead, you have to
depreciate the asset, assigning a proportion of the asset to the
Profit and Loss account and offsetting that amount against
any profits you make.

Depreciation is an accounting method used to gradually
reduce the value of a fixed asset in the accounts. (Otherwise
known as *writing down your assets*). Depreciation applies a
charge through the Profit and Loss account and reduces the
value of the asset in the Balance Sheet.

If you have many different types of assets, figuring out individual depreciation amounts can become quite time-consuming.
Fortunately, Sage has a Fixed Asset Register that enables you
to enter the details of each asset (refer to Chapter 3 for more
on assets) and the method of depreciation you intend to use.
Each time you run your month-end option, Sage calculates the
depreciation due for each asset and automatically posts this
to the appropriate accounts.

Writing down your assets

Sage provides two accepted methods of calculating depreciation and a write-off facility; if you use the Fixed Asset Register, Sage calculates the depreciation for you.

Some people prefer to depreciate their assets manually by posting a nominal journal each month. In fact, for those of you who don't have Accounts Plus or Accounts Professional, that is exactly what you have to do, as fixed asset records aren't available in the Accounts entry-level program. (Perhaps you should have spent that extra bit of money!)

You can choose your method of depreciation, but after you have, you must use the same method consistently every year. This method becomes part of your Accounting Policy and is referred to in the Notes to the Accounts section of your year-end accounts if they are prepared by your accountant.

Your accountant can help you decide which of the methods I explain in the next sections is best for you.

Ruling on the straight line method

In *straight line depreciation,* the value of the asset is depreciated evenly over the period of its useful life. For example, an asset depreciated over a four-year period has a quarter of the value depreciated each year (25 per cent). The same amount of depreciation is charged each month. For example, an asset that cost £24,000 and is due to be depreciated over a four-year period is depreciated by £6,000 each year, which equates to £500 per month.

Counting down the reducing balance method

An asset is depreciated by a fixed percentage in *reducing balance depreciation,* but the calculation is based on the net book value (NBV) each year, so the NBV reduces each year. For example, a £12,000 asset with a four-year lifespan, depreciated at 25 per cent by using the reducing balance basis, is depreciated as shown in Table 15-1.

The *net book value* is the cost price of the fixed asset less the accumulated depreciation to date. So at the end of year one, a £12,000 asset has depreciated by £3,000 (at 25 per cent), leaving the net book value as £9,000.

Table 15-1	Depreciation on a £12,000 Asset over Four Years	
Year	**Net Book Value**	**Depreciation Amount**
1	£9,000	£3,000
2	£6,750	£2,250
3	£5,062.50	£1,687.50
4	£3,796.88	£1,265.63

Using the reducing balance method means that the asset never fully depreciates. The amount of depreciation just gets smaller and smaller each year. You're more likely to write off the asset because it's obsolete before the NBV is anywhere near to zero.

Going for the one-time write-off

If you use the *write-off* method, you make a single posting to write off the remaining value of the asset in one go. You may choose to write off an asset if you disposed of it and need to remove the value from the books. Alternatively, if the asset is so old that it's no longer worth the value shown in the books, it's a candidate for write-off.

Posting assets and depreciation

You post the actual capital cost of an asset when you make the invoice or bank payment and you've coded the item to Fixed Assets. You make the depreciation postings when you run month-end routines or if you've chosen to manually post your journals each month-end. You can only make the postings once in a calendar month. For those using the month-end option (which I explain later in this chapter), if you forget to run the depreciation, you need to set the program date back to the month that you forgot to run and post the depreciation.

For those of you posting your depreciation journals manually, the double-entry way to complete your journals is to debit Depreciation (an expense account in the Profit and Loss) and credit Accumulated Depreciation (a Balance Sheet account).

To make sure that you're posting the correct amount of depreciation, you need to check that your Fixed Asset records are up to date. Ensure that you correctly set up the asset and the required depreciation.

Entering Journals

If you don't have Accounts Plus or Professional, pay special attention to this section, as it explains what journals actually do. You need to understand the principles of double-entry bookkeeping to make journal entries competently.

A *journal* is where you transfer values between nominal accounts. You can use journals to correct mistakes where something was posted incorrectly, but you don't use journals just for corrections. For example, you use journals to do your accruals and prepayments if you don't want to use wizards.

You use debits and credits to move values between nominal accounts. The journal must balance, so you need equal values of debits to equal values of credits, otherwise Sage is unable to post it.

I suggest using journals only if you're confident with double-entry bookkeeping. Otherwise, just stick to the wizards, because they perform the double-entry for you.

You may need to update several journals on a monthly basis, including depreciation journals if you're not using the Fixed Asset Register, wages journals and any other journals that you may require to correct items posted to the wrong account (cleverly known as *mispostings*).

To complete a journal, follow these steps:

1. **From the Company module, click New Journal from the Task pane or the Journals icon.**

2. **Enter the necessary information in the Nominal Ledger Journal sheet.**

   You're asked for the following information:

- **Reference:** For example, 'June 2010 depreciation' if you're manually posting depreciation and not using the Fixed Asset Register.

- **Posting Date:** The system uses the current day's date, so you need to specify the date on which you want to post the journal.

- **Nominal Code:** Use the dropdown arrow to select the first nominal code for your journal.

  For example, if you're posting a journal for depreciation, you may show a debit entry for Plant and Machinery (N/C 0020) for the sum of £200. The detail would read 'P&M June Depreciation'. The corresponding credit entry would use Plant and Machinery Accumulated Depreciation (N/C 0021) for the sum of £200, as shown in Figure 15-1.

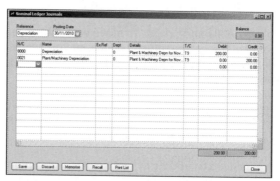

Figure 15-1: An example of posting a journal for depreciation.

- **Name:** The nominal code name automatically comes up on the screen.

- **Extra Ref:** Since Sage 50 2011, a new column has been added for you to provide extra detail, should you wish to.

- **Department:** Choose a department if you need one.

- **Details:** Enter details of the journal to appear on the Nominal Activity report.

- **Tax Code:** The system defaults to T9, the code most often used, but you can change this if required by using the dropdown arrows.

- **Debit or Credit:** Fill in the appropriate column according to whether it's a debit or a credit.

When you finish, the Balance box shows zero and the totals of the debits and credits is the same.

3. **Click Save if you're happy with the journal.**

The journal is posted to the nominal codes shown.

Prior to saving the journal, you have the option to reverse it at a future point in time. This is particularly useful if you're posting an accrual or prepayment type of journal. Tick the box Reverse Journals and then enter the date that you want the journal to reverse on. These boxes only show up on your nominal journal if you've ticked the box Enable Reversing Journals on the Parameters tab of Company Preferences (accessed from the main toolbar).

Rattling skeleton journals

If you do the same journals on a regular basis, you can take advantage of the option to create a *skeleton journal,* which you can reuse. After you save a skeleton journal, when you need to use the journal, all you do is recall it, and the details that you saved appear.

You can only save values in your skeleton journals if you tick the Copy Skeleton Journal Values box in Settings⇨Company Preferences⇨Parameters.

Creating a skeleton journal

You enter the journal details as described in the preceding section, but instead of saving the journal, click Memorise. The Memorise box opens, and Sage prompts you for a file name and a description of the journals. Type these and then click Save, which saves the journal for reuse another time.

Recalling a journal

When you're ready to reuse your skeleton journal, from Company, click Journals to bring up the Nominal Ledger journal. Click Recall to see a list of memorised journals. Highlight the journal you want and click Load. The journal comes up on the screen, as if you'd just entered it. If you want to make changes to it, you can overtype the details.

Reversing journals

Sometimes you may want to cancel a journal. Making a mistake when you're trying to reverse a journal manually is very easy, especially if you get the double-entry wrong. Sage can help you with the reversing journal option.

The main reason you may want to reverse a journal is because you got the double-entry bookkeeping wrong – maybe you got your debits mixed up with your credits – easily done! As long as you can identify both the debit and the credit that need to be corrected and these have individual transaction numbers, you can reverse them. You may not need to reverse the whole thing; perhaps just two lines of your original journal need reversing.

Before you undertake the nominal journal reversal, take a backup – just in case things go wrong and you need to restore the data. You must also be sure which transactions you want to reverse.

To carry out the reversal, from Company, click Reversals. At this point, Sage prompts you to take a backup and print a copy of the Nominal Ledger Daybook report, which I advise you to do. Next, click OK and a new box appears, where you enter the transaction range your journal appears in. (You can find this information on the Nominal Ledger Daybook report that you printed.) Enter the date of the original journal and then click OK. A Nominal Reversal window opens, showing the journal transactions that you want to reverse. Highlight the items for reversal and click Reverse, followed by Save.

If the journal you're trying to reverse doesn't come up, check that you used the correct transaction number. Also make sure that the journal you're trying to reverse balances, otherwise Sage doesn't accept the reversal. Now that you've reversed the offending journal, don't forget to post the correct one!

The journal you reversed shows on the audit trail with the reference REVERSE and the details say, 'Reversal of transaction XX'.

Carrying Out Your Month-End Routine

Running the month-end process in Sage allows you to automatically run the accruals, prepayment and depreciation journals described in earlier sections. However, you also get the opportunity to clear your customer and supplier month-to-date turnover figures, remove fully paid and reconciled transactions, clear the audit trail and remove stock transactions – although the last two tasks are optional.

The month-end process gives you the opportunity to review your accounts and prepare for the next accounting period. After you post all the journals and run all monthly routines, you can start running reports (which I cover in Chapter 17).

Ticking off your checklist

Having a checklist is probably the easiest way to run the month-end in a controlled manner. Use the following month-end checklist to ensure that you do everything.

Prior to running the month-end, run through these tasks:

❑ Change your program date to the month-end (Settings➪Change Program Date).

❑ Enter all transactions for the current period.

❑ Process bank recurring entries for the month.

❑ Reconcile all bank accounts (including credit cards).

❑ Post all journals (including skeleton).

❑ Post revaluation journals if you use foreign currency.

❑ Set up prepayments, accruals, fixed assets and depreciation.

❑ Post opening and closing stock journals (use
Modules⇨Wizards⇨Opening Closing Stock Wizard).

❑ Take a backup and label it. For example, 'June 10
month-end'.

As you run month-end processes, be sure to cover these
points, as necessary:

❑ Remove stock transactions if required.

❑ Clear audit trail if required.

❑ Take another backup entitled 'After month-end' with the
date.

As you work through the month-end processes, be sure to tick
off each item, so that you can see which tasks are remaining.

Running the month-end

The month-end procedure allows you to clear down the
month-to-date turnover figures on all your customer and supplier records. In clearing the month-to-date turnover figures,
Sage zeroes down the sales or purchase value in the Month
to Date field, which helps for reporting purposes. And, if you
have Accounts Plus or Accounts Professional, you can process your accruals, prepayments and depreciation as well.

You can post transactions beyond the month-end date, and
Sage designates them to the appropriate month. Even after
you post the month-end, you can still post transactions to
any previous accounting period: Sage just slots them into the
appropriate month.

To run the month-end, follow these steps:

1. **Click Tools⇨Period End Tools⇨Month End from the
main toolbar to bring up the Month End window.**

2. **Select the appropriate options by putting a tick in
the relevant boxes in the Month End window.**

   Ticking the Clear Turnover Figures box sets your
   month-to-date turnover figures for your customers
   and suppliers to zero.

You can post prepayments and accruals that you previously set up, as well as the depreciation for assets set up with the Fixed Asset Register.

3. **Click OK if you're happy to run the month-end.**

4. **Click Yes when the confirmation message appears to complete the month-end process.**

Alternatively, you can click Manage Month End from the Company screen, which takes you through the checklist items in the preceding 'Ticking off your checklist' section, using the appropriate wizards.

Clearing stock transactions

Clearing stock transactions is a way of reducing the number of transactions that appear on your product activity ledger. You clear the transactions up to a date you specify. You may decide to do this if your system is beginning to slow down due to the vast number of records it has to process. A year-end is often a good time to clear stock transactions. You don't have to clear the stock transactions, and many people prefer not to, as they like to be able to view a complete history of transactions.

You must print off your Product Valuation and Product Activity reports prior to clearing your stock transactions.

When you run the Clear Stock option, it removes all individual product transactions from each product record, leaving Adjustment In (AI) and Movements In (MI) – records of stock movements – which are brought forward as opening balances.

You can clear your stock from the main toolbar. Click Tools⇨Period End⇨Clear Stock. A confirmation message appears, asking if you're sure that you want to continue – click Yes. Sage then asks for a date to clear transactions up to. Enter the date you want and click OK to continue or Cancel to exit. Transactions prior to that date are permanently removed from stock transaction history.

Clearing the audit trail

The process of clearing your audit trail actually removes fully paid and fully reconciled transactions from the audit trail up to a date that you choose. You're left with fewer transactions on the screen, which makes it easier to work with and also speeds up the process of running reports and backing up your data.

Taking backups prior to running this process is absolutely essential. Clearing your audit trail is irreversible. Make sure that you print your audit trail, daybook reports, sales, purchase and nominal activity reports, and also any VAT return reports prior to running the Clear Audit Trail option.

You can look at the deleted transactions by clicking Company⇨Financial Reports⇨Cleared Audit Trail Reports (from the Links list).

During the process of removing transactions, Sage posts journal entries to the nominal codes to which the transactions were linked. This posting ensures that the balances on the nominal accounts stay the same as before the Clear Audit Trail process was run. The journals are displayed with the detail opening balance and appear at the end of the audit trail when the Clear Audit Trail process is complete.

To run the Clear Audit Trail, simply click Tools from the main toolbar and then Clear Audit Trail. A wizard opens, which takes you through the process step by step. Click Next to work through each screen. On the final screen, you need to click Process to begin the Clear Audit Trail process. When the process is complete you're shown how many transactions were removed, and you can view the cleared transactions. If you want to see the removed transactions, tick the I Would Like To View Details Of The Removed Transactions box to open the Audit Trail Historic List report. You can print or save this report if you desire.

Doing a Year-End Routine

The year-end procedure is principally a financial accounting process. You must run your month-end for the last month of your accounting year, which takes care of the usual journal routines (although you are probably a little more careful at checking things like accruals and prepayments at the year-end).

The year-end procedure clears down the Profit and Loss accounts to zero and transfers any current-year profit or loss to the Retained Profit account. You carry forward the balances on the Balance Sheet to the new year and transfer any future-dated transactions into the relevant months for each nominal record.

As regards budgets, you transfer the actual values for the current to the prior year, so that you can make comparisons in the new financial year.

You must make sure that you take a backup before you run this process (Sage recommends taking two, so that if one is lost or damaged, you always have another copy). You also need to check that you've run all the reports that you require for your accounts and that you've adjusted your system date to the same as your year-end date (Settings➪Change Program Date).

Check that your Chart of Accounts doesn't contain any errors, although you should notice these sorts of mistakes when you run your Profit and Loss and Balance Sheets for the year.

To run your year-end, follow these steps:

1. **From the main toolbar, click Tools➪Period End➪Year End.**

   The Year End window appears.

   Alternatively, you can select the Manage Year End option on the Company toolbar. This wizard takes you through the process step by step.

2. **Select Copy Current Year Budgets for both your nominal and departmental budgets and also your stock budgets.**

   You can increase your budget by a percentage increase if desired.

3. **In the Postings box, enter the date you want on your year-end journals.**

   Your financial year-end date appears here automatically, but you can change it if you want to.

4. **Decide what method of output you want for your year-end updated audit trail – you can print or save it to a file.**

5. **Choose whether to archive the closing year's data. To archive, select the Archive Company Data Before Year End check box.**

6. **After you're happy with the details that you've chosen, click OK.**

   Sage now continues with your year-end.

You may want to take a backup and label it 'After the year-end'. You can also check the data.

Before you begin the next financial year, check that the financial year start date is correct (Settings⇨Financial Year). Click OK if the details are correct.

You've now completed your year-end!

Chapter 16

Running Your VAT Return

*T*he letters VAT (which stand for Value Added Tax, of course) usually have a profound effect on people, from grown men turning a pale shade of green to a pure state of panic if a VAT inspection suddenly looms! You can avoid all this by keeping proper accounting records with a system such as Sage and running your VAT returns in a systematic, methodical manner.

The actual running of a VAT return takes seconds, due to the integrated nature of the Sage software, but you need to check it properly as I outline in this chapter.

Understanding Some VAT Basics

You only need to worry about VAT if your business is VAT registered. After you register, you can reclaim VAT on certain purchases, but you also have to charge and pay VAT across on your sales.

Your company can voluntarily register for VAT and should if you can reclaim VAT on a significant proportion of your purchases. VAT registration is mandatory if you exceed certain

VAT thresholds – currently, you must register if your annual sales reach £70,000 or above.

A basic knowledge of what you can claim VAT on and what you can't pays off (literally!). You can find many books on this subject, and the VAT office also provides plenty of publications for specific industries. A quick look on the HM Revenue and Customs (HMRC) website at www.hmrc.gov.uk gives you a list of all publications. You can find the main VAT rules and procedures in Notice 700.

Knowing your outputs from your inputs

VAT inputs and outputs have nothing to do with the Hokey Cokey. I wish they were that enjoyable!

Output VAT is just a fancy name for the VAT element of your sales. *Input VAT* is the opposite; it represents the VAT element of your purchases.

Basically, a VAT return compares the total of your VAT inputs and outputs, and subtracts one from the other. If the outputs exceed the inputs, you owe the Revenue, and if the Inputs exceed the Outputs, then the Revenue owes you a refund! Yes, it does happen. . . .

Cracking the codes

When you enter invoices, credit notes or orders (whether for your customers or suppliers), you need to know which tax code to use. Sage automatically provides you with a list of UK tax codes, or T codes:

- ✔ **T0:** Zero-rated; VAT is not payable on zero-rated supplies. Examples include books, children's clothes and some items of food.
- ✔ **T1:** Standard rate; currently 20 per cent.
- ✔ **T2:** Exempt from VAT. For example, postage stamps.
- ✔ **T4:** Sales to customers in the European Union (EU).

✔ **T5:** Lower-rate VAT, usually 5 per cent; this applies to the purchase of energy-saving materials and, for example, reclaiming VAT on DIY building work.

✔ **T7:** Zero-rated purchases from suppliers in the EU.

✔ **T8:** Standard-rated purchases from suppliers in the EU.

✔ **T9:** Transactions not involving VAT. For example, wages.

Comparing Sage's VAT accounting methods

Sage supports three types of VAT schemes: the standard VAT accounting scheme, VAT cash accounting and more recently the flat rate VAT scheme. The Inland Revenue provides some helpful information about the VAT schemes available on its website; if you want to find out more, go to www.hmrc.gov.uk.

Set up your accounting method before you enter any transactions onto Sage. The Active Set-up wizard I talk about in Chapter 1 includes the accounting method as one of its steps. If you're not sure which method you chose, click Settings⮕Company Preferences and then click the VAT tab. In the VAT details box, you'll find the VAT scheme that has been selected. You can use the drop-down arrow to view the other VAT schemes that Sage supports. The next sections explain these three methods.

Setting the standard scheme

In the standard VAT scheme, Sage calculates the amount of VAT based on when an invoice is issued. Therefore, as you raise each invoice, you're liable to pay the VAT on it when your next VAT return is due. However, you can reclaim the VAT on invoices sent to you from your suppliers, regardless of whether you've paid them or not.

Considering cash accounting

VAT cash accounting calculates the VAT based on when your customer pays an invoice and when you pay your supplier. You benefit if your customers are slow to pay, as you don't need to pay the VAT across until they pay you.

VAT cash accounting in the Republic of Ireland is slightly different. Sometimes known as the *monies received* scheme, you calculate your VAT on the money you actually receive from customers and on the invoices or credits you receive from your suppliers. Sage 50 Accounts has the ability to operate both the UK scheme and the Republic of Ireland scheme.

Figuring out the flat rate VAT scheme

The flat rate VAT scheme allows you to pay VAT as a fixed percentage of your VAT inclusive turnover. You don't claim VAT back on any purchases, making it a very simple system to operate. The actual percentage you use depends on what type of business you're in.

You can only join the flat rate scheme if your estimated VAT taxable turnover (excluding VAT) in the next year will be £150,000 or less. You can then stay on the scheme until your business income is more than £230,000.

Sage enables you to set up both invoice and cash-based flat vat rate schemes.

Running the VAT Return

Running a VAT return in Sage is remarkably easy, *but* – and it's a big but – you have to check your VAT return before you send it in.

To access the VAT ledger, from Company, click Manage VAT from the Task pane. You can see the VAT Return icon here; this provides you with both detailed and summary reports of the VAT on both sales and purchases, and calculates what you owe to HMRC or how much you're due to be refunded.

Also included within the VAT ledger are icons to help you calculate your fuel-scale charges, a wizard to help you complete VAT transfers (both outlined later in this chapter), print EC sales lists, make VAT payments, produce a reverse charge Sales list and finally, a selection of tax analysis reports that you can run.

When figuring your VAT, an appreciation of what items VAT is charged on and what types of items you can reclaim VAT on helps. If you're unsure, contact your accountant or HMRC for help.

Before you start figuring out your VAT return, make sure that your books are up to date for that period. By this, I mean enter all sales invoices and purchase invoices and all receipts and payments, and reconcile all the bank accounts and credit card accounts to ensure that you've accounted for all elements of VAT.

The first step of running your VAT return is to calculate the amount owing or owed. The calculation is easy to do; just follow these steps:

1. **From Company, click Manage VAT in the Task pane to open up the VAT window.**

   Alternatively, you can click Financials from the Company Links list and then click VAT from the Financials screen.

2. **Click the VAT Return icon.**

   The VAT form opens up. This form looks like the manual VAT return that you get from HMRC.

3. **Enter the period that the VAT return relates to.**

   For example, 01.06.10 to 31.08.10.

4. **Click Calculate.**

   Sage tells you how many transactions were found for this VAT return, as well as how many transactions are dated before the specified period but haven't been reconciled. You can choose whether you want to include them or not. If you choose not to include them, they remain as unreconciled items in the audit trail and appear again when you do your next VAT return.

5. **Click OK to continue.**

   As soon as you click OK, the VAT Return fills with figures, and you can see how much Sage thinks you owe the Inland Revenue or vice versa.

Figure 16-1 shows a VAT return for Jingles. Sage found 43 transactions, including fifteen unreconciled transactions before the specified period. In the example, these unreconciled item are included as they form part of the set-up of the company and need to be accounted for. Sage calculates that Jingles owes £221.51 to HMRC.

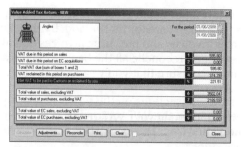

Figure 16-1: A standard VAT return for Jingles.

Checking Your VAT Return

You may think that the job is done after Sage calculates your VAT. However, the information is only as good as the person who entered it, so you need to check it against the information held in the nominal ledger. The checks are different depending on which VAT scheme you operate. I look at each scheme in turn and examine which reports you need to check to ensure the accuracy of your return.

Checking under the standard scheme

Your Sales Tax and Purchase Tax control accounts must agree with the boxes on the VAT return. To make sure that they do, print the VAT return, a detailed VAT report and the Nominal Activity report for both the Sales Tax control account and the Purchase Tax control account. These documents identify all elements of VAT on sales and purchases. Make sure the Nominal Activity report is run for the same quarter period as the VAT return.

Printing out the VAT return and a detailed report

The main screen of the VAT return is the place to go to print VAT reports. Just click Print and a VAT Return Report window opens. Tick both the VAT Return and Detailed boxes and then click Run. Sage previews both reports on the screen, one behind the other. The screen behind the VAT return has a white background and has lost the green colour – don't worry, this is normal. Print a copy of both reports.

The detailed VAT report provides a breakdown of all the transactions behind each number on the VAT return. And, if you use the VAT standard accounting scheme, the detailed VAT report shows each sales invoice and credit note, and every purchase invoice and credit note.

Sage groups the transactions on the report according to the box they belong in on the VAT return. For example, you can see each individual transaction contained within VAT box 1.

Getting a hard copy of the Nominal Activity report

You need to check that the net value of the Sales Tax control account and Purchase Tax control account on the Nominal Activity report agree with box 5 of the VAT return. To check, print the nominal activity for codes 2200 and 2201, the Sales Tax control account and the Purchase Tax control account.

If the net value of the tax control accounts doesn't agree with box 5, do the following checks:

✔ Make sure that you selected the same dates for the Nominal Activity report as you have for the VAT return. That way, you select data for the same period and it should agree, unless you've said Yes to any unreconciled items from a previous quarter.

✔ Check if the VAT control accounts include any totals for tax codes that aren't included in your VAT return. For example, T9 by default isn't included in your VAT return.

✔ Check that your Clear Down journals have been correctly posted from the previous quarter. (I talk about these journals in the 'Clearing Down VAT' section later in this chapter.)

✔ See if any journals were posted to the VAT control ledgers. Journals don't normally need to be posted to the control accounts, so if they are, you need to fix that error.

✔ Check the audit trail. You can check which items have already been reconciled by looking for *R* for reconciled in the V (VAT) column. Those with an *N* in the column haven't been reconciled and need checking as part of the current VAT return.

✔ If you still can't find the discrepancy, print the Customer daybook reports and the Supplier daybook reports and manually tick off each item to the tax control accounts. This last-resort check can be extremely time-consuming, but it does usually work.

✔ If you still have a discrepancy after all this, print the daybooks for your bank, cash, credit receipts and payments, and check these reports to find the error.

Checking with cash accounting

If you're operating the VAT cash accounting system and working from a cash-based system instead of an invoice-based one, you need to print several reports. First, print your detailed VAT report as described in 'Printing out the VAT return and a detailed report' in the previous section. Then follow these steps:

1. **From the navigation bar, click Company⇨Financials from the Links list.**

   The Financials window opens.

2. **Click the Audit icon and select Detailed. Click Run.**

   The Criteria box opens.

3. **Select the same quarter period as your VAT return and then click OK.**

   Your report appears in Preview format. Click Print for a hard copy.

   Transactions that have an *N* in the V (VAT) column haven't yet been reconciled and are the transactions that you include in your current VAT return. Items with an *R* in this same column have been reconciled for VAT purposes and aren't included in the VAT return.

4. **Make sure that you use the same date range as your VAT return to print nominal reports.**

   The reports you print are:

   • **Nominal Ledger Daybook reports:** From the navigation bar, click Company, click the Reports icon and double-click Nominal Daybook Reports. Select Day Book: Nominal Ledger and the Criteria Value box opens. Select the same dates as your VAT quarter and click OK.

- **Customer Receipts and Supplier Payments:**
  Print these reports from Bank reports. These
  are all bank and cash accounts. (If you're using
  the Republic of Ireland VAT accounting scheme,
  you don't need to print the Supplier Payments
  report.)

- **Customer Invoices and Credits Daybook
  reports:** Print these reports from Customers.

- **Supplier Invoices and Credits Daybook reports:**
  Print these reports from Suppliers.

5. **Make sure that your VAT return is correct by checking
   it against all the reports you print in Steps 2, 3 and 4.**

Analysing Your VAT Return

After you calculate your VAT return, you can analyse it.

If you look at your green stripy VAT return, you can see the
numbers 1 to 9. Each number represents a line on the VAT
return. By clicking each box with a pound value in it, you
can drill down the VAT return and obtain a breakdown of all
entries made to each tax code, indicating if each entry is a
sales invoice, credit note, journal, receipt or payment. You
can also see any manual adjustments that have been made.

If you want even more detail, you can double-click any of the
numbers on the VAT Breakdown screen and view all the transactions that make up that total. You can click Print List to
obtain a detailed VAT breakdown. Click Close to return to the
VAT Breakdown screen and Close again to exit the screen.

Making Manual Adjustments
to Your VAT Return

Sometimes you miss something from your VAT return from a
previous quarter and you need to make an adjustment. In the
past, you had to get your biro and calculator out and make an
adjustment on the face of your VAT return prior to sending it

to HMRC, but now you can do it within Sage. Just follow these steps:

1. From the VAT Return, click Adjustments.

The VAT Manual Adjustments screen opens, as shown in Figure 16-2.

Figure 16-2: Making manual adjustments on your VAT return.

2. Click the arrow in the Adjustments column, and, in the screen that appears, enter some text describing why you're making the adjustment.

For example, your notation may be something like, 'prior quarter adjustment'.

3. Click Save.

You're returned to the previous summary screen, where you can now see your adjustment.

4. Click Close.

The VAT Return screen appears. The total amount owed to the Inland Revenue has now been revised for the manual adjustment that you just made. Sage posts the manual adjustments to the nominal default code 2204.

If you make an adjustment but close the VAT return without reconciling, the adjustments aren't saved.

5. Click Close again to return to the Financials screen.

Reconciling Your VAT Transactions

After you're happy with the information in your VAT return, you need to flag each individual transaction for VAT so that an *R* appears in the VAT column of the audit trail and it doesn't appear again in future returns, unless you ask to include previously reconciled transactions. This process is known as *reconciling your VAT return*.

To do the reconciliation, you must first calculate the VAT return for the correct VAT quarter. When you can view the VAT Return screen, click Reconcile. A confirmation message appears, asking you if you want to flag the transactions for VAT. Click Yes and then click Close.

To check if the transactions have definitely been reconciled, try to calculate the VAT return again for the same period. A message appears saying that you've selected a date range that's already been reported on. Click Yes to continue. Sage then confirms that no transactions were found for that period; evidence that the transactions have been reconciled. You can also check that the individual transactions have been reconciled by viewing the Audit Trail screen and looking for an *R* in the VAT column.

When you reconcile the VAT return, a copy of it is archived in Sage. The reconciled and archived VAT return is then listed on the VAT ledger window. It is given a return number as a method of identification. The listing shows the period of the return, the amount and has a Paid column that shows an *N* if the return hasn't yet been submitted to HMRC.

You can view a saved return by highlighting the return you want to view from the VAT ledger and clicking View. If you want to, you can delete the VAT return from Sage by highlighting the return and clicking Delete. However, you more than likely want to keep a copy of your VAT return on Sage. I recommend that you keep a hard copy of all your VAT returns and keep them somewhere safe. You must keep copies for the purposes of any VAT inspection for at least six years.

Submitting Your VAT Return

When you've reconciled your VAT return, you're ready to submit it to HMRC. You must keep a copy of all your reports, just in case you're inspected at a later point in time – HMRC has six years to do so. You must also enable e-VAT submissions on your VAT preference settings – click Settings⇨Company Preferences⇨VAT tab and tick the e-VAT Submissions box.

HMRC prefer you to send your VAT return online, so to send your online VAT return, follow these steps:

1. **From the VAT Ledger screen, highlight the VAT return you want to send.**

   The return's status must be pending or partial.

2. **Click Submit Return.**

   Assuming your VAT preferences and e-submission credentials are set up correctly, the Sage Internet Submissions wizard guides you through the process.

You must have a Government Gateway account to make e-VAT payments. Go to www.hmrc.gov.uk for details on how to obtain one.

Clearing Down VAT

If you're wondering what on earth clearing is all about, don't worry, it's quite straightforward. Essentially, *clearing* is transferring the values from your Sales Tax and Purchase Tax control accounts to your VAT Liability account.

The balance created in your VAT Liability account should agree with the amount due to HMRC, or in the case of a reclaim, it should equate to the refund due.

After you make the VAT payment or refund (and post it to the VAT Liability account), the balance on the Liability account becomes zero.

If you're thinking that this sounds rather complicated, then panic not, as Sage has a wizard to help you! You can run the wizard from the VAT Ledger screen by clicking the VAT Transfer icon and following the instructions on screen.

After you transfer the values to the VAT Liability account and the VAT payment or refund has been received and posted to the account, the balance on that account is zero until the next clear down.

Changing VAT schemes

Can you change from VAT cash accounting to standard or flat rate accounting or vice versa? The answer is yes, you can, but you have to prepare carefully for the change.

Sage has a great Help facility which can assist you in the transition between your VAT schemes, so make full use of it by clicking on Help on the main toolbar.

Posting Scale Charges

Fuel-scale charges occur when company vehicles are subject to private use. According to HMRC, if fuel is bought by employees for business use and that vehicle is also used privately, the business must account for output tax on the private use by using scale charges.

If you use scale charges, you can claim back all the VAT charged on road fuel without splitting your mileage between private and business use. The calculations are based on the CO_2 emissions of the vehicle plus the engine size.

Scale charges only apply to cars and not to commercial vehicles.

Thankfully, Sage has made claiming back VAT much easier with a wizard that guides you through the process. You can access this wizard from the main toolbar by clicking Modules, then Wizards, and selecting Scale Charges Wizard. Sage makes the postings, and you can view the entries on your VAT return.

Before you continue with the wizard, you need to calculate the scale charge for each vehicle. The HMRC publication Notice 700/64 helps you do this. You can get a copy from the HMRC website at www.hmrc.gov.uk.

Reporting Intrastat

Intrastat is concerned with collecting statistics surrounding the physical movement of goods around the European Union. It's closely linked with the VAT system, and if you're not VAT registered, you don't have any obligations under the Intrastat system. However, if you exceed the so-called assimilation threshold in the amount of goods you supply to customers in the EU, you're required by law to submit certain details about your trade to HMRC. You can find details about Intrastat in HMRC Notice 60 – 'Intrastat General Guide'.

You have to complete Supplementary Declarations (SD) forms, which Sage can help you prepare. You then transfer the information from Sage onto the official SD forms.

You need to submit a European Community (EC) Sales List if you're VAT registered and supply products to Customers in the European Union. The information on the lists is used by the UK and other member states to ensure that the appropriate amount of VAT has been calculated. For up-to-date details about the rules relating to the EC Sales List, check out the HMRC website (www.hmrc.gov.uk).

For information about Intrastat reporting and how Sage can help, press F1 and type **Intrastat** into the Sage Help function.

Chapter 17

Running Monthly Reports

. . . .

In This Chapter

▶ Using the Sage standard reports

▶ Using the Chart of Accounts to check report layouts

▶ Running a Trial Balance

▶ Creating a Profit and Loss account

▶ Printing your Balance Sheet

▶ Viewing the audit trail

▶ Writing reports

. . . .

*T*his chapter concentrates on the reports that you can produce at the end of the monthly accounting procedure. I assume that you've run the month-end procedure and processed all the necessary journals, as I tell you how to do in Chapter 15. Now you need to provide some meaningful information to the managers of the business. The reports must be easy to understand and use headings that are meaningful to the business.

Running reports is an opportunity to see how well your business is progressing: if the business is meeting targets set earlier; if you're bringing in as much revenue as you'd projected and how actual costs compare to the budgeted or forecasted expenditures.

Making the Most of the Standard Reports

Whenever possible, use the standard reports provided by Sage, as they're simple to run and provide most of the information that you need.

Each ledger contains its own reports. For example, you go to Customer and then Reports to see the Aged Debtors report or Customer Activity, or you go to Bank and then Reports to see reports such as a copy of the unpresented cheques. The Financials module houses the Profit and Loss report and Balance Sheet – the key financial reports that tell you how the business is doing. You find these by clicking Company and then Financials (on the Links list), and then selecting the appropriate icon on the Financials screen. You can find more information about these reports and how to run them later in this Chapter.

Usually at a month-end or year-end, the accountant prepares a set of management reports to present to the owners and managers of the business. I explain these reports in upcoming sections.

Checking the Chart of Accounts First

You must check the Chart of Accounts (COA) for errors before you run financial reports as errors in the COA can affect the accuracy of the reports. (Refer to Chapter 2 for more information on the COA.) If you try to run a balance sheet without checking, you're likely to get a message saying that errors exist in the Chart of Accounts and that the reports may be inaccurate as a result. And no one likes having a machine tell them they're wrong!

To check the COA for errors, click COA from the Company module, highlight the COA you want to check, click edit and then click the Check box. If there are no errors, Sage advises you of this. If there are errors, Sage allows you to print or preview the errors.

Figuring Out the Financial Reports

The reports that give you a view of the business-end of your business are the Trial Balance, Profit and Loss and Balance Sheet reports. You generally run each report at the end of the accounting period, whether that's every month, every quarter or annually. I cover each report in the following sections.

Trying for an initial Trial Balance

This report doesn't show up in a pretty layout – it's basically a list of numbers in nominal code order, and numbers are rarely lovely to look at – but the Trial Balance forms the basis of your Profit and Loss and Balance Sheet reports, so it's very important.

In this report, you see a list of all debit or credit balances in nominal code order for the period you specify – you have to specify a month, and Sage presents the balance at that time. The report only shows nominal codes that have a balance, so any codes with a zero balance don't make the list. As the example in Figure 17-1 shows, the debits and credits are in separate columns with totals at the bottom of each. Because of the double-entry bookkeeping principles (mandating a debit for every credit), the two columns balance.

Date:	15/01/2011		Jingles		Page:	1
Time:	11:13:19		Period Trial Balance			
To Period:	Month 12, March 2011					
N/C	**Name**			**Debit**	**Credit**	
0020	Plant and Machinery			5,000.00		
1001	Stock			400.00		
1100	Debtors Control Account			3,772.84		
1200	Bank Current Account			3,808.95		
1205	Bank of America			978.43		
1206	Bank of Japan			1,050.52		
2100	Creditors Control Account				2,176.74	
2200	Sales Tax Control Account				595.80	
2201	Purchase Tax Control Account			374.29		
3020	Capital Introduced				6,500.00	
3100	Reserves				100.00	
3200	Profit and Loss Account				5,071.39	
4000	Sales of Greetings Cards				279.60	
4010	Sales of Balloons				25.00	
4150	Party Organising				3,100.00	
4902	Commissions Received				55.00	
5000	Purchase of cards			852.50		
5015	Purchase of Party Gifts			286.00		
5150	Party Organising Costs			1,000.00		
7000	Gross Wages			130.00		
7004	Wages - Regular			250.00		
			Totals:	17,903.53	17,903.53	

Figure 17-1: Jingles' Trial Balance for the period ended in March 2011.

Jingles is still quite a new company and doesn't have many transactions yet, nor does it use many nominal codes. As business increases, the number of codes – and hence the Trial Balance – increases in length.

In a Trial Balance, you can see at a glance the extent of your assets and liabilities and use it as an investigative tool. For example, if something seems out of whack, you can run more detailed reports to see where the numbers came from. For example, the Jingles' accountant is interested in finding out why £5,000 is posted to Plant and Machinery and runs a Nominal Activity report to investigate further.

You can run a Trial Balance from Company by clicking Financials from the Links list. If you then click the Trial icon, the Print Output box opens, and you can select Preview and then click Run. The Criteria box opens, and you can use the dropdown arrow to select the period you want to view. In the example in Figure 17-1, I used March 2011.

Accounting for profit and loss

Owners and directors of businesses really like the Profit and Loss report (or at least they should do) because it shows them if they're making any money! The Profit and Loss report shows the total revenue (sales) that your company has made in the specified period and then deducts both direct costs and overheads for that same period to arrive at a profit or loss for the period.

The layout of the Profit and Loss report is a standard format, but you can use the Chart of Accounts function to rename headings and group together your nominal codes so that the Profit and Loss report appears with terminology suited to your business. (Refer to Chapter 2 to see how to edit your Chart of Accounts.)

You can run your Profit and Loss report from the same Financials page as the Trial Balance (see the preceding section) – click the P and L icon. You should select the Print Output that you want and then click Run. You have a choice to print, preview, send to a file or email – previewing first is wise, so that you can see if you're happy with the report criteria you chose. The Criteria box then opens. Select the period for which you want to run the report by filling in the From and To dates and use the dropdown menu to select a Chart of Accounts layout other than the default (refer to Chapter 2 for information on adding new COA layouts). Click OK, and the Profit and Loss report appears. It's split into two columns, one showing the current period and the other showing the year-to-date (YTD).

Be aware that if you select a full year as your From and To dates, you end up with both columns showing the same figures. If you choose a single month (for example, June) in the criteria, the Period column then differentiates the current period (June) from the year-to-date figures. Of course, the numbers for the first month of the year and the YTD numbers are the same!

In Figure 17-2, the From and To dates are the same (both August 2010, the fifth month of the business year) so the Profit and Loss report shows just the month of August. The year-to-date (YTD) figures aren't very different, which tells you that the majority of Jingles' business was done in the month of August – probably a fair representation with a new business.

| Date: 15/01/2011 | Jingles | Page: 1 |
| Time: 11:21:51 | Profit and Loss | |

| From: | Month 5, August 2010 | | |
| To: | Month 5, August 2010 | | |

| Chart of Accounts: | Default Layout of Accounts | | |

		Period		Year to Date	
Sales					
Shop Sales		0.00		304.60	
Party Fees		3,000.00		3,100.00	
Other Sales		0.00		55.00	
			3,000.00		3,459.60
Purchases					
Purchases		726.00		1,138.50	
Purchase Charges		1,000.00		1,000.00	
			1,726.00		2,138.50
Direct Expenses					
			0.00		0.00
	Gross Profit/(Loss):		1,274.00		1,321.10
Overheads					
Gross Wages		130.00		380.00	
			130.00		380.00
	Net Profit/(Loss):		1,144.00		941.10

Figure 17-2: A Profit and Loss report for Jingles.

Weighing the Balance Sheet

A lot of people don't understand what a Balance Sheet tells them, but it's a useful tool for establishing the financial position of a company because it provides a snapshot of the business at a point in time. The Balance Sheet shows the assets and liabilities and the sources of funds that helped finance the business. From a Balance Sheet, you can see how much money is owed to the business and how much the business owes.

The Balance Sheet forms part of the management accounts of the business and is traditionally issued at the month-end, quarter-end and year-end. Some people prefer to issue just one set of accounts at the year-end, but others prefer a more regular source of information and require monthly accounts.

You can access the Balance Sheet from the Financials page by clicking Balance Sheet. Select Preview, and then click Run, and the Criteria box opens up. You can use the dropdown arrow to select the period From and To that you want to view. If you have more than one Chart of Accounts layout, select the one you want to preview (refer to Chapter 2 for details on setting up additional Charts of Accounts).

The Jingles example in Figure 17-3 uses Month 5 August to Month 5 August 2010 for a snapshot of August's numbers.

Make sure that you understand the component parts of the Balance Sheet. For example, can you agree your debtors figure in the Balance Sheet to an Aged Debtors report? Do you understand what transactions are included in the accruals and prepayments? You can check all figures by looking at your Chart of Accounts and determining which nominal codes represent each section of the Balance Sheet. You can then print a Nominal Activity report to see what transactions are included. To run this report, click Company, Reports and then Nominal Activity Reports.

Figure 17-3: Balance Sheet for Jingles as at 31 August 2010.

Looking at Other Reports

Sage offers many other reports, including Budget reports where you can compare Actual spend against Budget spend. You can also compare current year expenditure against prior year expenditure. (Some companies use prior-year data to establish if they're doing better than last year.) You can find these reports in the Financials module. Sage also offers plenty of other reports which you may want to have a play around with to see what takes your fancy!

Viewing the Audit Trail

The *audit trail* is a list of all the transactions that have ever occurred in Sage, including those subsequently deleted. So when you make a complete mess of something, rest assured that you can never escape it. It's there for all to see – even your accountant and the auditor, who may use it at year-end!

Sage lists the transactions in the audit trail chronologically and each has a unique transaction number. This number is used alongside a search tool to find a particular transaction, which is useful if you need to correct a specific transaction.

You can clear the audit trail periodically to remove the details of the transactions, but the balances are kept and carried forward so that the accounts remain accurate. You can find an explanation of this routine in Chapter 15. However, Sage has the capacity to hold 2 billion transactions in the audit trail, so you don't actually ever have to clear it down if you don't want to.

You get on the audit trail through the Financial module. You can click the Audit icon to explore further. The Audit reports are available in brief, summary, detailed and deleted transactions. The first three reports show the transactions in varying levels of detail; the last shows exactly what it says – transactions you deleted from the system. The report lists a line per transaction, so if you have thousands of transactions, the whole report can be extremely long!

To run the audit trail, follow these steps:

1. **From Company, click Financials and then the Audit icon.**

   The Audit Trail Report window opens.

2. **Enter your choice of audit report – brief, summary, detailed or deleted transactions. Then choose the method of output and click Run.**

   The Criteria box opens.

3. **Choose the criteria required for this report.**

   Sage recommends that you run this report on a monthly basis, so enter the current month dates.

4. **Click OK to generate the report.**

   If you choose to preview the report, providing you're happy with the way it looks, you can print, export or email it from this screen.

5. **Click Close to exit the report and return to the Financials screen.**

You usually print off the audit trail at the end of each period, and it provides a hard copy of all business transactions. Often, it's printed at the year-end to provide a copy for the auditors, but it's up to you how regularly you decide to print it. Obviously the longer the period, the longer the report.

Figure 17-4 shows an extract from a brief Audit Trail report for Jingles.

Figure 17-4: An extract from the Audit Trail report – the brief version.

Designing Reports to Suit Yourself

Sometimes you need to personalise one of the many standard reports Sage offers. You can change the existing layouts to suit yourself by using Report Designer.

Designing reports is a huge topic, and Sage used to have a separate reference book just to deal with report writing. I don't delve into this subject here; I just scratch the surface.

The easiest place to start is by finding a report that almost matches your needs, but not quite. You can then take this report, save it under a different file name and reconfigure it with information that suits your business needs.

Sage has a great Help facility to assist you in creating your reporting requirements. You can access this feature by using F1 from within the Report Browser in Sage 50 Accounts.

Part V
The Part of Tens

'Now we've got all this money, we're going to need a sensible accounting system.'

In this part . . .

This last part includes a detailed look at how function keys can help you speed up data processing and a demonstration of the wonderful ways wizards work their magic to help you with both the basic setting up of records and also some of the trickier aspects of bookkeeping.

Chapter 18

Ten Funky Functions

In This Chapter

▶ Getting help

▶ Finding out about shortcuts

▶ Opening programs

*I*f you want to wow your friends (or your boss) with a few neat tricks, then look no further than this chapter! Here, you find out how to use some of the function keys that give you some great shortcuts – for example, the copy key (F6), which speeds up processing no end and F7, which can get you out of a tight spot if you need to insert an extra line somewhere (particularly useful if you've missed a line of information from the middle of a journal). Read on to find out more.

Browsing for Help with F1

Pressing F1 launches the help system. The system is intelligent enough to know which part of the system you're working in and displays the Help screens most suited to your needs. In doing so, it saves you having to scroll through the Help index list to find the appropriate section. For example, if you're in the Batch Entry screen for suppliers, pressing the F1 key brings up a Help screen related to entering purchase invoices.

Calculating Stuff with F2

Having instant access to a calculator is pretty handy, particularly if you're in the middle of a journal and you need to add something up. Simply press your F2 function key, and a little calculator appears on the screen. You can quickly do your sums and then carry on processing information using Sage, without having to dive through your office drawers trying to find the calculator.

Accessing an Edit Item Line for Invoicing with F3

Pressing F3 displays the Edit Item line when you're entering invoices. You can add additional information and comments to your invoice, whether a product or service invoice.

Note: you need to enter some information first before the Edit box will open.

Finding Multiple Functions at F4

Pressing this button does different things depending on which screen or field you're in:

- ✔ In a field that has a dropdown arrow, press F4 to display the full list.
- ✔ In a Date field, press F4 to show the calendar, instead of clicking the Calendar icon.
- ✔ In a numeric field, press F4 to make a mini-calculator appear, instead of clicking the Calculator icon. (F2 opens a calculator in any screen, F4 opens one only if you're in a screen devoted to numbers.)

Calculating Currency or Checking Spelling with F5

The F5 key has dual purposes:

- ✔ It shows the Currency calculator when the cursor is in a numeric box. (*Note:* you need to ensure that your currencies and exchange rates are set up for this to function.)
- ✔ It brings up the spell checker when the cursor is in a text box.

Copying with F6

F6 is one of the best inventions ever! It copies entries from the field above, which is particularly useful when you're entering batch invoices (for both customers and suppliers). For example, if a batch of invoices all have the same date, you can enter the date once, and, as you enter each subsequent invoice, press F6 when you get to the Date field. Sage copies the date from the field directly above your line of entry and enters the same date into the invoice on the line of the batch that you're working on. You can do this for any of the fields. So, if you're entering a mass of invoices from the same customer or supplier, you can use F6 to copy the details from one invoice to the next. This function has an amazing impact on the speed of data entry, and it's an absolute godsend when you set up a new system, as you often have a lot of data entry to do.

Inserting a Line with F7

The ability to add a line may seem pretty mundane and boring, but it's very useful when you're entering batches of invoices or journals. You can be halfway through entering a journal and realise that you've missed out a line. Instead of putting it at the bottom of the journal, you can press F7 to insert a line where you want it.

Deleting a Line with F8

F8 is one of my favourite function keys. Many a time, I've got to the bottom of a very long and laborious journal and been a bit carried away. Before realising it, I've started to enter an extra line of journal that shouldn't be there.

After you enter a nominal code, Sage expects you to continue to post that line of the journal and waits for you to enter a value. When you realise your mistake and try to save the journal with a zero amount on the last line, Sage doesn't allow you to post. It gives you a warning message, saying `No transaction values entered`.

But click the line you want to delete, press F8 and it miraculously disappears, allowing you to save the journal with no further problems.

Many a student has told me that they've got to that point and, not realising what to do, have ended up discarding the original journal and retyping it all!

The F8 key can be used in other parts of the system too, for example, when you want to delete a line from an invoice or order.

Calculating Net Amounts with F9

When entering an invoice, Sage asks you for the net amount of the invoice, followed by the tax code. After you enter the tax code, Sage calculates the VAT. If you don't know the net amount and only have the gross amount of the invoice, you can type the gross amount in the Net field and press F9. Sage then calculates what the net amount is.

Launching Windows with F11

F11 launches the Windows control panel. Having access to the control panel is useful, for example, if you accidentally send a report to the printer. To cancel the job, press F11. The control panel opens and you select the Printer icon. Double-click the printer where the job is waiting to print and delete the report from the queue. Click the black cross in the right corner to exit the control panel. Alternatively, you can configure this button to launch another program. Use the Help menu for instructions on how to do this.

Chapter 19

Ten Wizards to Conjure

In This Chapter

▶ Looking at how wizards can help you perform tricky transactions

▶ Scanning the more helpful wizards and how they work

*S*age helpfully provides a number of *wizards*. No, I don't mean little characters with pointy hats and wands. By wizards, I mean step-by-step instructions on how to carry out specific procedures. Sometimes they can be a bit long and laborious to use, but at other times they provide some much needed expertise. For example, they can help you to complete complicated journal entries – even the most dedicated book-keepers can do with a bit of help sometimes!

Here, I provide a brief summary of the most helpful wizards that Sage offers.

Creating a New Customer Account

Using the navigation bar on the left side of your screen, click Customers and then New Customer in the Task pane. The New Customer wizard starts, taking you step-by-step through the twelve-window process of setting up your customers. As the wizard can take a long time, I use the quicker method of clicking Customer and then Record, but you may prefer the wizard's guidance, so make sure that you grab a cuppa first!

To have a look at the type of questions that you're asked as you work through the wizard, press the F1 function key. The Sage Help facility describes in detail the type of information you need to enter in each of the twelve windows.

Setting up a New Supplier

Using the navigation bar, click Suppliers and then New Supplier in the Task pane. The New Supplier wizard walks you through the process of setting up your supplier records, just as the New Customer wizard takes you through setting up your customer records – wizards are handy, but not too imaginative. The eleven windows you complete help you set up supplier names, addresses, contact details, credit details, bank details and settlement discounts, if applicable.

To preview the types of information required to complete the wizard, have a look at Sage Help. Press the F1 function key and scroll up and down the screen to see for yourself.

You don't have to complete every field in the wizard to set up a supplier, but you do need to click through all eleven windows to get to the end and save what information you've entered, so stick with it! You can always add information to your supplier record at a later date if you feel that you've missed anything out – simply open the supplier record, make your changes and click Save – it's that easy!

Initiating a New Nominal Account

Use the Nominal Record wizard to create new nominal accounts to use in your Chart of Accounts. You only need to work through five screens – what a relief! From the navigation bar, click Company and then the New icon, which starts the wizard for you. The wizard asks you to enter the name of your new nominal account and confirm what type of account it is – sales, purchase, direct expenses, overheads, assets, liabilities and so on. The next screen asks you to enter your nominal category from within the Chart of Accounts – for example, product sales. It also asks you to type in your nominal code.

Save yourself some annoyance and decide on your nominal code before you start the wizard. At this point in the wizard, you don't have the option of searching your nominal code list to check if your chosen code is suitable.

The wizard asks if you want to post an opening balance. Click the appropriate answer, and then click Next to continue. That's it! You've reached the final screen, and you've successfully entered the details for your new nominal account. When you click Finish, the new record is created and any opening balances are posted to it.

Don't forget to check your Chart of Accounts for any errors after you enter new nominal accounts. You can find details on how to do this in Chapter 2.

Creating a New Bank Account

The Sage New Bank Account wizard enables you to open new bank accounts, but is a long process. The first four windows ask the usual bank details, such as bank name, sort code, account number and so on. The last few windows concern your opening balances and entering details about them.

From the navigation bar, click Bank, and then click the New icon.

Launching a New Product

Use the New Product wizard to create a new product record. You're asked to enter descriptions of the product, selling price and cost price information, as well as nominal codes and supplier details. It also has a section on opening balances that allows you to enter those through the wizard.

To access the wizard, from the navigation bar, click Products and then click the New icon. Alternatively, you can click New Product from the Task pane on the navigation bar, instead of clicking the New icon.

Starting Up a New Project

You can use the New Project wizard to create a new project record. (Chapter 13 talks in more depth about creating projects to keep track of a job's progress.) You're asked to enter details such as the project name and unique reference, which can be just a shortened name or number to identify the project. Enter information such as the project start date and end date and choose a status from the five pre-defined ones Sage that provides. If you can link the project to a customer, enter those details. The next couple of windows are optional and contain questions such as the site address and site contact details. The last-but-one window requires you to enter the price you quoted for the project.

To access the Project wizard, click the New icon from the Projects module, or click New Project from the Task pane on the Projects navigation bar.

Helping Out at Month End: Opening/Closing Stock

Click Modules from the main toolbar, and then click Wizards. Choose Opening Closing Stock Wizard to access this wizard, which forms part of the month-end routine and is a welcome method of recording your closing stock. The wizard records the amount of closing stock you have at the end of a period and then transfers it to the start of the next period. The theory is that by recording your opening and closing stock figures, the cost of sales figures can be accurately calculated by the wizard for your Profit and Loss report. (Cost of Sales = Opening Stock + Purchases × Closing Stock.) If you don't post opening and closing stock figures, the cost of sales only reflects the purchase cost and doesn't reflect stock that you have left to sell. Work through all four screens, entering the required information and clicking Next to proceed to the end of the wizard.

The wizard asks you to confirm the closing stock nominal accounts in both your Balance Sheet and the Profit and Loss report. At the Entering Your Closing Stock Values screen, Sage requests you to enter the values of the closing stock and that of the previous closing stock value. Sage then calculates the double-entry bookkeeping and posts those entries when you click the Finish button.

Fuelling Up: Scale Charges

If your firm has lots of company car users, the Scale Charges wizard can come in handy. It enables you to calculate the fuel-scale charges levied against free fuel provided to employees using company cars for personal use. Charges are dependent on the carbon-dioxide emissions and engine-size of each car.

You're required to enter the fuel-scale charge details. Sage creates the journals necessary to post to the nominal ledger.

Before you proceed with the wizard, you need to have calculated the scale charge for each company vehicle. You can find this information on the scale-charge table provided by HM Revenue and Customs Public Notice 700/64; go to www. hmrc.gov.uk.

Helping with Your Bookkeeping: VAT Transfer

Known as the VAT Liability Transfer wizard, this wizard sounds very complicated, and it can be if you don't understand double-entry bookkeeping. (Have a look at *Bookkeeping For Dummies,* by Paul Barrow and Lita Epstein for more help on double-entry.) This wizard helps you create the VAT transfer journals necessary to clear down your VAT Liability account. Still as clear as mud? Read on.

Essentially, the double-entry system reverses the balances in both the Sales Tax control account and the Purchase Tax control account at the end of the quarter and places an equal and opposite entry in the VAT Liability account. In theory, the balance subsequently created in the VAT Liability account is equal to the amount owed at that quarter-end. Therefore, when the VAT has been paid across or reclaimed from the VAT office for the quarter and that payment or refund is coded to the VAT Liability account, the balance on the VAT Liability account should be zero – assuming that you've done all the bookkeeping correctly. Phew! The wizard makes going through this process a breeze.

You can't use this wizard until you've fully reconciled and printed your VAT return.

Handling Currencies: Foreign Trader Set-up

You have to complete the Foreign Trader Set-up wizard to activate the foreign currency functionality in Sage Accounts Professional.

After you activate the Foreign Trader option, you can't switch it off!

To activate the Foreign Trader, from the main toolbar, click Modules⇨Wizards⇨Foreign Trader Set-up Wizard.

The Foreign Trader Set-up wizard is short but sweet. It runs for only four screens, but the impact of activating it is huge. The wizard first asks you to set up a new nominal account to handle currency fluctuations. When dealing with foreign currencies, you often encounter different exchange rates between sending invoices and receiving payment from them. These different rates result in slight under- or overpayments on accounts, and a foreign currency fluctuation account is an account to post those under- or overpayments to. If you've selected the default range of nominal codes, an exchange-rate variance code already exists, which you can use.

Sage also asks you which exchange-rate update method you want to use. You can change exchange rates on individual transactions, but it may be better to update the currency record as well. Sage recommends that you use the default offsetting, which always prompts you to save exchange-rate changes so that you can keep on top of things when you change a record. The other exchange-rate update options include automatically saving exchange-rate changes to the currency record and never saving exchange-rate changes to the currency record.

When you complete the wizard, Sage recommends that you check the currency codes, symbols and currency exchange rates before you continue any further. Wise words!

Index

deleting, 160
Details tab, 148–149
duplicating, 150–151
editing, 150, 151–152, 157–158
Footer Details tab, 149–150
main body, 149
Order Details tab, 149
placing goods on order, 151–152
printing, 153–154
receiving goods, 154–158
receiving part delivery, 157–158
un-cancelling, 161
updating, 151, 158–159
purchase order processing (POP),
    150, 151, 153, 157, 185–187
Purchase Tax control account,
    227, 232, 255

• *Q* •

quick start option, 35–36, 37–39
quotation, 129–132

• *R* •

rebuilding data, 119
recalling
    batch invoices/credit notes, 93
    skeleton journal, 213–214
    stocktake, 164
receipts, uncleared, 60–61
reconciling VAT return, 231. *See
    also* bank reconciliation
record
    creating, 35–37
    customer, 37–39, 251
    fixed asset, 52–53
    importing, 16
    product, 47–50, 253
    project, 50–51, 253–254
    searching for, 121–123
    supplier, 37–39, 252

recording. *See* entering
recurring entries, 88, 107–110
reducing balance depreciation,
    209–210
Reference field
    bank deposits and payments, 105
    bank reconciliation, 197
    batch entry invoices, 68
    journal, 212
    petty cash, 112
    purchase invoice, 159
    purchase order, 148
    supplier invoice, 94
reference number, 181
registering
    Sage 50 Accounts, 12
    for VAT, 221–222
re-indexing data, 118
Remember icon, 4
remittance advice slip, 71, 99–100
renaming
    bank account, 44–45
    Chart of Accounts headings, 31
    nominal record, 40–41
    project status categories, 178,
        179, 180
report. *See also* Balance Sheet
    Aged Creditors, 58, 60, 94
    Aged Debtors, 57, 60, 236
    Audit Trail, 242–243
    bank reconciliation, 204
    Budget, 241
    designing, 243–244
    management, 236
    Nominal Activity, 227, 240
    Product Writeoff Details, 172
    Profit and Loss, 25, 27–28,
        31, 236, 238–239
    project, 189
    project cost, 189
    Shortfall, 166
    standard, 236
    Trial Balance, 237–238

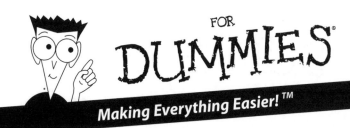

Making Everything Easier!™

UK editions

BUSINESS

Marketing Kit FOR DUMMIES

978-0-470-74490-1

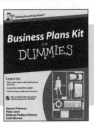

Business Plans Kit FOR DUMMIES

978-0-470-74381-2

PRINCE2 FOR DUMMIES

978-0-470-71025-8

REFERENCE

British Politics FOR DUMMIES

978-0-470-68637-9

DIY FOR DUMMIES

978-0-470-97450-6

Researching Your Family History Online FOR DUMMIES

978-0-470-74535-9

HOBBIES

Growing Your Own Fruit & Veg FOR DUMMIES

978-0-470-69960-7

Allotment Gardening FOR DUMMIES

978-0-470-68641-6

Electronics FOR DUMMIES

978-0-470-68178-7

Anger Management
For Dummies
978-0-470-68216-6

Asperger's Syndrome
For Dummies
978-0-470-66087-4

Boosting Self-Esteem
For Dummies
978-0-470-74193-1

British Sign Language
For Dummies
978-0-470-69477-0

Cricket For Dummies
978-0-470-03454-5

Diabetes For Dummies,
3rd Edition
978-0-470-97711-8

Emotional Healing
For Dummies
978-0-470-74764-3

English Grammar
For Dummies
978-0-470-05752-0

Flirting For Dummies
978-0-470-74259-4

Football For Dummies
978-0-470-68837-3

Healthy Mind & Body All-in-One
For Dummies
978-0-470-74830-5

IBS For Dummies
978-0-470-51737-6

Improving Your Relationship
For Dummies
978-0-470-68472-6

Nutrition For Dummies,
2nd Edition
978-0-470-97276-2

Available wherever books are sold. For more information or to order direct
go to www.wiley.com or call +44 (0) 1243 843291

24940 (p1)

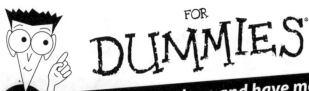

FOR DUMMIES®

The easy way to get more done and have more fun